Acknowledgments

The study was coordinated by Don Blayney and Mary Anne Normile of USDA's Economic Research Service. The coordinators gratefully acknowledge the contributions of David Anderson, Texas A&M University; Joseph Balagtas, University of California-Davis; Scott Brown, University of Missouri; Oral Capps, Texas A&M University; Tom Cox, Bob Cropp and Hooman Dabidia, University of Wisconsin; Thomas Fiddaman, Ventana Systems, Inc; Ken Hanson, USDA, ERS; Hal Harris, Clemson University; Ron Knutson, Texas A&M University; James Miller, USDA, ERS; Mitch Morehart, USDA, ERS; Charles Nicholson, Cornell University; Victor Oliveira, USDA, ERS; Joe Outlaw, Texas A&M University; J. Michael Price, USDA, ERS; James Richardson, Texas A&M University; Robert Schwart, Texas A&M University; Sara Short, USDA, ERS; Mark Stephenson, Cornell University; Daniel Sumner, University of California-Davis; and Cameron Thraen, Ohio State University. The authors express sincere thanks to Mary Bohman, USDA, ERS; Dan Colacicco, USDA, FSA; Neilson Conklin, USDA, ERS; Ralph Dutrow, USDA, FAS; Anne Effland, USDA, ERS; Bruce Gardner, University of Maryland; Larry Hamm, Michigan State University; Jay Hirschman, USDA, FNS; James Johnson, USDA, ERS; Jeff Kahn, USDA, OGC; Paul Kiendl, USDA, FAS; Milton Madison, USDA, FSA; Lynn Maish, USDA/OBPA; Alden Manchester, (retired) USDA, ERS; Jim MacDonald, USDA, ERS; Howard McDowell, USDA, AMS; John Mengel, USDA, AMS; James Miller, USDA, ERS; Janet Perry, USDA, ERS; Larry Salathe, USDA, OCE; Scott Steele, USDA, OBPA; Richard Stillman, USDA, ERS; Daniel Sumner, University of California-Davis for their valuable review comments; to Chris Dicken, Lou King, and Anne Pearl, USDA, ERS, for editorial and design assistance; and to Coco Clayton, Lewrene Glaser, Agnes Prentice, and LaVerne Creek, USDA, ERS, for their work to produce the compact disc version of the report.

Contents

Overview

The U.S. Congress, in the Farm Security and Rural Investment Act of 2002 (the 2002 Act), directed the Secretary of Agriculture to conduct a "comprehensive economic evaluation of the ... effects of the various elements of the national dairy policy." The Act further directed the Secretary to study the effects of (a) terminating Federal milk price support and supply management programs, and (b) allowing State cooperation to manage milk prices and supply. Both studies deal with similar questions that relate to the effects of government policies on economic outcomes. For this reason, the two studies are combined into this single report.

This report examines the effects of national dairy policy and its component programs as defined in the 2002 Act on milk and dairy product markets, farm households, nutrition programs, and the rural economy.[1] These programs include:

- Federal milk marketing orders,
- the Federal milk price support program,
- State pricing programs and State-mandated over-order premiums,[2]
- interstate dairy compacts,[3]
- direct payments to milk producers, and
- the dairy export incentive program (DEIP).

The report focuses on the following questions: what have been the measurable effects of dairy programs on economic variables—price level and volatility, milk production, and producer revenues? How have these market impacts in turn affected farms, rural economies, and nutrition programs? How might States cooperate to support prices in the absence of a Federal price support program? The standard tools of economic analysis are used to address these questions, but there are also other forces at work that have influenced the dairy sector. Changes in the dairy sector should be considered in a larger context with a longer-run perspective. Thus, the first part of this report answers another, related question: what factors can we identify that have been responsible for changes in the dairy sector?

Dairy Policy in the Context of Structural Change

Many of the individual programs that make up U.S. dairy policy were originally designed to deal with the industry's structure in the 1930s, when most milk production (60 percent) was destined for fluid consumption, markets were predominantly local, and many dairy enterprises were part of diversified farming operations. Today, the largest share of milk is used for manufactured dairy products (especially cheese) rather than fluid milk; markets for manufactured dairy products are national in scope; and dairy farms are highly specialized, many of them large-scale industrial-type farms.

Production technologies that provide economies of scale have led to increased specialization and to consolidation on both sides of the farmgate. On the farm, milk yields per cow have increased steadily as a result of genetic improvement, better herd management, and adoption of technolo-

[1]Programs identified in the 2002 Act are primarily domestic. Because the Act did not request an analysis of the effects of trade measures—and to better isolate the effects of dairy programs on the U.S. industry—current levels of import protection for dairy products are assumed to remain in place.

[2]The qualifier "State-mandated" has been added by the authors to distinguish over-order premiums regulated by State dairy programs from market-generated over-order premiums that are not part of any dairy program.

[3]Interstate dairy compacts are not part of current dairy programs.

gies that promote output growth. For example, over the last 40 years, milk yields have grown even faster than corn yields, with an average annual rate of growth of 2.2 percent compared with 1.8 percent for corn (fig. 1.1). With milk yields growing faster than milk consumption, fewer cows are needed to meet milk demand, leading to a decline in the size of the U.S. dairy herd. Fewer cows, coupled with increased economies of scale, led to a decline in the number of U.S. dairy farms of more than 70 percent between 1980 and 2003, while average herd size more than tripled (fig. 1.2).

Figure 1.1
Milk yield per cow outpaces corn yields

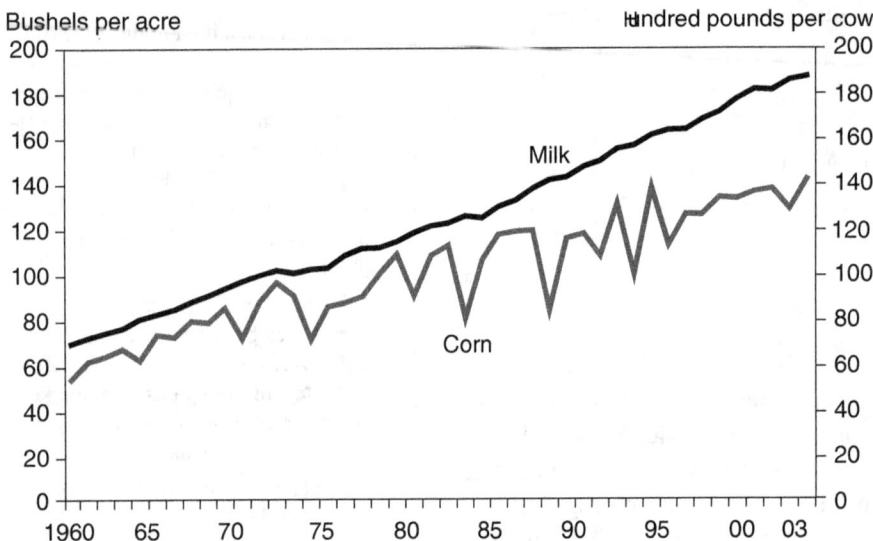

Source: USDA, ERS from USDA, NASS data.

Figure 1.2
Dairy farm numbers decline while average herd size grows

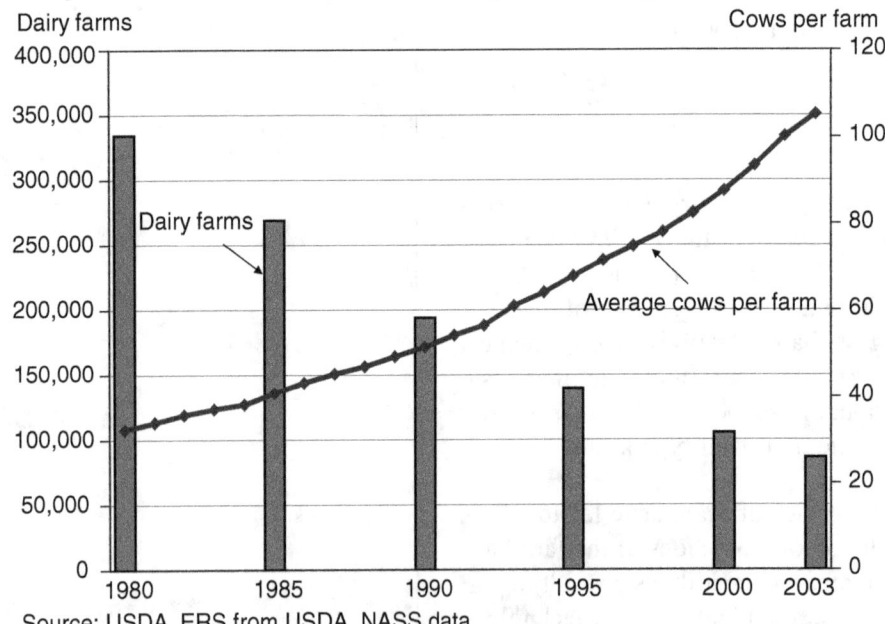

Source: USDA, ERS from USDA, NASS data.

Change in the dairy industry has varied across the United States over the past several decades. Dairy product markets have become essentially national in scope, driven by advances in transportation and processing technologies. Similar factors have expanded fluid milk markets, although fluid production still tends to be located close to major consumption areas. Milk production overall has shifted from traditional milk producing areas (close to 20th century population centers) to areas with an underlying comparative advantage in milk production. Less expensive land, favorable climate that permits large-scale operations with lower housing costs, the availability of high-quality and low-cost feed, access to hired labor, and proximity to major new markets for dairy products have all contributed to a westward shift in the U.S. dairy industry (fig. 1.3). While milk production for fluid use remains concentrated near large population centers, production of milk for manufacturing uses is increasingly located in low-cost areas— the West and Southwest. Manufactured product plants follow milk production, and as milk production has expanded in western areas, so have new, large-scale cheese plants.

Dairy Policy Has a Modest Impact

Seventy years of Federal intervention in dairy markets makes it difficult to quantify the full impacts of national dairy policy, since it is not possible to know how today's industry would look in the absence of dairy programs. However, economic models simulating the effects of removing current dairy programs provide broad insights into dairy policy's implications for milk producers, consumers, and the rural economy.

An examination of dairy program impacts suggests that Federal dairy programs raise the all-milk price by only about 1 percent, and raise total producer revenues (returns plus government payments) by 3 percent, on

Figure 1.3
Milk production shifts West

Change in milk production by farm production region, 1980-2003

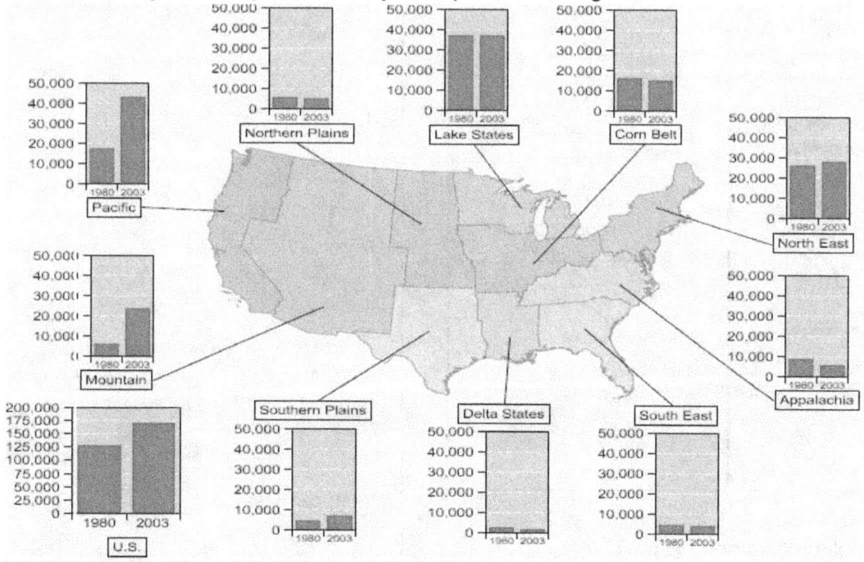

Note: Units are million pounds of milk.
Source: USDA, ERS from USDA, NASS data.

average, over 5 years. Shortrun effects of policy can be significantly larger. Estimated effects of government programs would also be greater in years of low prices. While producers are, as a whole, better off with dairy programs, these programs do raise consumer costs (modestly) and increase government expenditures.

Dairy programs can have countervailing effects. For example, the Milk Income Loss Contract (MILC) program, by increasing producer returns through production-linked payments, expands production and thereby reduces the milk price. Without the MILC program, the remaining dairy programs raise the all-milk price by 4 percent (compared to about 1 percent with MILC), on average, over 5 years.

Because they have modest effects on prices and returns, Federal dairy programs have a limited impact on profitability and viability of dairy farms, increasing the share of farms that cover all costs by 5 percent in the short run (fig. 1.4). By increasing farm-level returns, these programs may enable high-cost farms to remain in business longer, but only in the short to medium term. In the longer run, high-cost farms will have difficulty competing with low-cost dairy producers. Higher prices improve the profitability of low-cost dairy producers, which may enable them to expand production and gain market share.

The stability of prices and returns is especially important to dairy farms since they tend to be less diversified and more dependent on income from the farm business than other farms. An analysis of dairy program effects on the milk price suggests that price supports and the MILC program may lead to modestly lower price variability.

The effect of dairy programs on farms varies regionally. An analysis of dairy program effects on the financial conditions of representative farms

Figure 1.4
Dairy programs increase number of farms covering economic costs by 5 percent

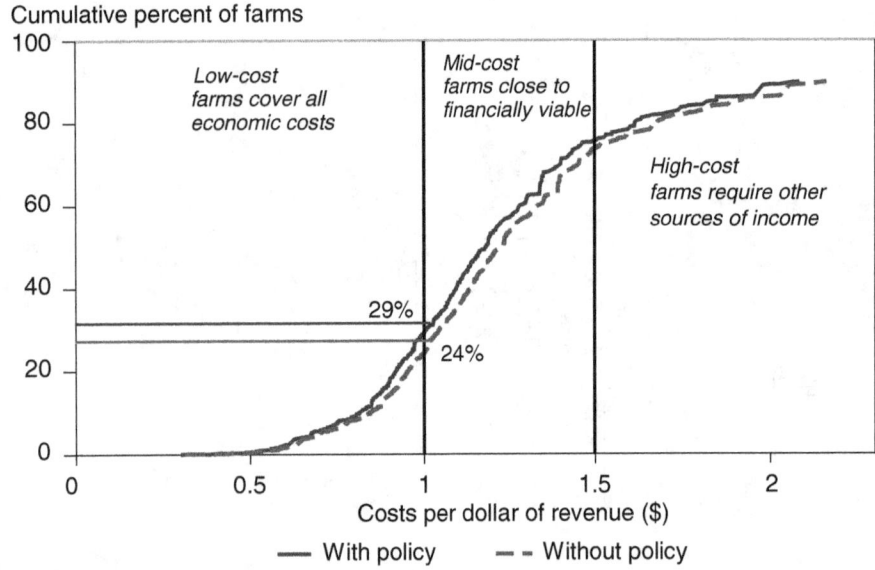

Cumulative percent of farms

Source: USDA, ERS from USDA, NASS data.

around the United States reveals that the current policy structure may lower the returns of some Western dairies.

Dairy programs raise the retail price of fluid milk and lower the prices of manufactured products such as butter and cheese. This affects both consumer expenditures on food and the cost of operating food and nutrition programs. The Special Supplemental Nutrition Program for Women, Infants, and Children (WIC) is a discretionary grant program funded by annual appropriations. The number of participants depends on the appropriation and the cost of operating the program. To the extent that dairy programs increase the retail price of fluid milk and other dairy products—products that make up a large share of the WIC food package—they have the potential to reduce program participation. Other food and nutrition programs are entitlement programs, and their costs are indexed to price indices that increase Government outlays when dairy programs raise product prices. Higher prices are therefore unlikely to affect participation. However, higher dairy prices can affect how Food Stamp recipients choose to spend their food dollars.

National dairy programs have almost no impact on aggregate economic activity. Both nationally and at a broad regional level, the industry's impact on employment is less than 0.1 percent of total employment. In areas that are highly dependent on milk production, impacts are likely to be greater. Because farm input (like machinery and fertilizer) production is located in metropolitan areas—as is much of the upstream processing and distribution activity—dairy programs very likely have greater impacts on metropolitan than on nonmetropolitan employment. Moreover, a comprehensive assessment of dairy programs' impacts on the national economy should consider the costs associated with additional taxes required to cover dairy program budgets.

State Management of Milk Supplies and Prices Raises Difficult Issues

Milk markets have a long history of State intervention. In the era when a city's milk supply was produced locally and milk markets were driven by fluid consumption, States had a greater ability to affect prices without running afoul of interstate commerce laws or contending with competition from other States. However, as milk markets have become increasingly integrated across State boundaries, the potential for effective State-level intervention in dairy markets has diminished. Today, of the major milk-producing States, only California and Pennsylvania set minimum prices for milk to any great extent.

Congress requested an analysis of State or regional market intervention as an alternative approach to Federal milk price support. The analysis extends the model of the Northeast Interstate Dairy Compact (NEIDC) by hypothesizing the formation of three interstate compacts grouped along the lines of existing Federal Milk Marketing Orders (FMMO) and roughly approximating regions proposed for Compact authorization in legislation introduced in both the 107th and 108th Congresses.[4] Other FMMO regions are assumed to remain outside the compacts. The study assumes that these compacts are imple-

[4]H.R. 1827, introduced May 14, 2001; S. 1157, introduced June 29, 2001; and H.R. 324, introduced January 8, 2003.

mented while eliminating the Federal milk price support program (there is no Federal supply management of milk), but all other programs—primarily MILC and Federal milk marketing orders—are assumed to remain in place. This scenario provides some general insights into the economic and policy issues associated with State and/or regional management of milk prices.

In general, compacts establish a minimum regional price that processors are required to pay for Class I milk, the milk used in fluid beverage products. When the compact price is greater than the FMMO price, the difference (or some share of it) is returned to producers selling milk in the compact region. Higher returns to these producers lead to increased milk production, and fluid milk consumption drops as consumers react to the higher retail prices. The resulting excess supply of milk above fluid requirements within the compact region spills over to the manufacturing milk market. As a result, manufacturing milk prices decline, as does the price of fluid milk in areas outside the compacts. These effects are greatest during low-price years.

As long as fluid utilization is high enough, returns to dairy farmers supplying the compact region increase as the higher fluid milk price more than offsets any decline in the price of manufacturing milk. However, lower manufacturing milk prices are felt nationally and returns to dairy farmers outside the compact region decline. Farmers in regions with higher levels of manufacturing use for their milk suffer the greatest losses because they receive no MILC payment to dampen the loss of revenues from fluid milk.

In this scenario, farmers in the Southeast compact region reaped the largest gains while milk producers in the Southwest and Arizona (non-compact regions) suffered the greatest losses. Direct payments under the MILC program would offset some of the impact on farmers outside the compact region.[5] Consumers both outside and within the compact region benefit from lower prices for manufactured dairy products. However, consumers within compact regions spend more on fluid milk, while consumers outside the compact region would spend less on fluid milk.

Thus, the general net effect of an interstate compact is to benefit dairy farmers within and consumers outside the compact region. The costs of the compact are borne by consumers within the compact region, by dairy farmers outside compact areas, and, in the event direct payments are continued, by taxpayers.

Compacts may provide regional price support, as long as a large proportion of production in the compact region is sold into the higher priced fluid milk market, but are unlikely to substitute for price support on a national level. Extending compacts across the entire country would increase the impact on national milk production. Without some form of supply control, higher fluid prices applied to all producers would induce increased milk production that would spill over to the manufacturing milk market, driving down the price of milk for manufacturing use even further. The average producer price across all uses would decline further, rendering price management efforts ineffective.

[5]The analysis assumed that MILC continued following the introduction of a compact.

This analysis raises questions regarding other means of State support. Were States to pursue a support program similar to the Federal milk price support program, States would need to address the issues of program funding, how price support levels would be established, and, if product purchase programs were implemented, the disposition of product stocks. If supply control programs were adopted, additional considerations include establishing and enforcing quota levels and penalties or incentives for compliance. Such systems raise questions regarding cross-border issues—how to deal with milk flowing to areas with different price support or quota levels. While State or regional management of milk prices has received considerable attention as a possible alternative to current policy, this analysis suggests that it likely raises even more difficult issues than current policy.

Conclusions

The analysis shows that effects of dairy programs on markets are modest and current dairy programs are limited in their ability to change the long-term economic viability of dairy farms.

Other forces—technology, changing consumer demand, and changes in the marketing and processing sectors—while difficult to measure, are likely more important to the future of the dairy industry.

While State or regional dairy policy approaches have received much attention, this analysis suggests that they may increase producer returns in States or regions that implement them, but can reduce returns elsewhere. Extending these approaches nationwide, in the absence of an underlying Federal milk price support program, is unlikely to increase producer returns without requiring supply control measures.

Future policies should include clearly defined goals to devise targeted measures that take into account underlying forces driving the transformation of the U.S. dairy sector.

Introduction

National dairy policy and the programs designed to promote it have been in existence in various forms for about 70 years. Dairy programs now include price support and product storage, import protection, marketing regulations that set minimum prices by use and pool revenues for producers, export subsidies, and direct producer payments. The dairy industry of today—from the farm level through processing, manufacturing, distribution to retailing—has been shaped in part by the mix of policies and programs in effect throughout its development.

The U.S. Congress, in the Farm Security and Rural Investment Act of 2002 (the 2002 Act), directed the Secretary of Agriculture to conduct a "comprehensive economic evaluation of the ... effects of the various elements of the national dairy policy." The Act further directed the Secretary to study the effects of (a) terminating Federal milk price support and supply management programs,[1] and (b) allowing State cooperation to manage milk prices and supply. (See Appendix A for the sections of the Act that comprise the mandate for the two studies.) Since both studies focus on similar questions that relate to the effects of government policies on economic outcomes, they are combined into a single report.

The 2002 Act defines "national dairy policy" to mean the dairy policy of the United States as demonstrated by the following programs:

- Federal milk marketing orders,
- the Federal milk price support program,
- State pricing programs and State-mandated over-order premiums,[2]
- interstate dairy compacts,[3]
- direct payments to milk producers, and
- export programs such as the dairy export incentive program (DEIP).

The 2002 Act also defines the primary questions to be addressed in this report:

- What are the effects of dairy policy on farms and rural economies?
- How do these policies affect government nutrition programs, participating institutions, and program recipients?
- What are the impacts of dairy policy on markets for dairy products?

Any attempt to evaluate the effects of dairy programs must recognize that forces other than national dairy policy have influenced the dairy sector's development and contribute to economic outcomes. Changes in demand; advances in production, transportation, and communication technology; the expanding scope of markets for dairy products; and productivity growth have been important factors. Consolidation at all levels of the industry can be explained by these forces and the incentive to reduce costs by exploiting economies of scale in a competitive industry. Many of these factors are responsible for regional shifts in milk production. The role of dairy

[1]There are currently no supply management programs for milk or dairy products in the United States.

[2]The qualifier "State-mandated" has been added by the authors to distinguish over-order premiums regulated by State dairy programs from market-generated over-order premiums that are not part of any dairy program.

[3]Interstate dairy compacts are not part of current dairy programs.

programs has at times been to support milk producer prices and/or incomes to help them deal with the impacts of some of these forces.

Observations of the changing structure of the dairy sector frequently underlie policy concerns. The extensive structural changes that have taken place throughout the U.S. dairy industry have been the result of many forces, not all policy-related. "The Evolution of the Modern Dairy Industry" assesses the forces influencing the dairy sector and, where possible, relates changes in the structure of the dairy industry to the interaction between dairy programs and other forces.

"Public Policy in the Dairy Industry" provides a brief description of the dairy programs covered by the study, and places them in the context of the evolution of U.S. dairy policies and programs. This chapter is intended to provide an overview of the operations of the programs that will be evaluated in subsequent chapters.

"The Effects of National Dairy Programs" presents the results of the analyses of the effects of four key Federal dairy programs. (State and regional dairy programs are addressed in "An Alternative Milk Pricing Approach.") A multifaceted approach to analyzing the effects of the dairy programs is necessary given the wide range of issues to be addressed. Model-based analyses provide quantitative estimates of the effects of dairy policy on market outcomes—price, revenue, production, and consumption. Several quantitative analytical frameworks are used to provide the model-based analysis in "The Effects of National Dairy Programs," including two farm sector models, a representative farms model, an Input-Output model, and a system dynamics model.

Because at least some national dairy programs have been in place for many decades, there are effectively no observations of the modern U.S. dairy industry in the absence of government policy.[4] Consequently, a modified "counterfactual" approach was used to derive estimates of dairy program effects. A simulation of the dairy industry without programs is compared with a baseline industry simulation that includes programs. Effects derived from the simulation results are then applied in other analytical frameworks to estimate program effects on representative dairy farms and subnational economies. The system dynamics model is used to evaluate changes in selected dairy programs as they relate to milk price volatility

"An Alternative Milk Pricing Approach" examines the implications of adopting an alternative mechanism for establishing minimum milk prices while at the same time eliminating the Federal milk price support program. In doing so, this chapter analyzes the effects of interstate compacts in general. An interregional model of the dairy sector is used to examine the effects of replacing the Federal price support program with a system of interstate dairy compacts, similar to the Northeast Interstate Dairy Compact (NEIDC). While there are numerous possible scenarios for interstate cooperation to manage prices, the NEIDC provides a historical model for cooperative efforts by States.

[4]While we have no observations of the U.S. industry in the absence of extensive dairy programs, the experience of policy reform in other countries may provide some insights. Australia's deregulation of their dairy industry is described in an ABARE report on the impact of an open market in fluid milk supply at: http://abareonlineshop.com/product.asp?prodid=12204. The U.S. International Trade Commission has reviewed this report in *Conditions of Competition for Milk Protein Products in the U.S. Market,* Investigation No. 332-453, Publication 3692, May 2004. ftp://ftp.usitc.gov/pub/reports/studies/pub3692.pdf, p. 4-44 through 4-47.

This report is a synthesis of the results of several studies by a team of dairy industry experts including personnel of the Economic Research Service (ERS) of the U.S. Department of Agriculture and researchers at several universities. The quantitative analysis of farm sector impacts was undertaken by ERS, using the Food and Agricultural Policy Simulator (FAPSIM), and by the University of Missouri Food and Agricultural Policy Research Institute (FAPRI) using the FAPRI dairy model (Price, 2004; Brown, 2003). The effects of dairy programs on farms were analyzed using the Farm Level Income and Policy Simulator (FLIPSIM) model developed at the Texas A&M University (Outlaw et al., 2003). The analysis of the effects of dairy programs on the volatility of dairy prices was performed using a System Dynamics model developed at Cornell University (Nicholson and Fiddaman, 2003). Impacts of dairy programs on rural economies were developed by ERS using an Input-Output model (USDA, ERS, 2004). The analysis of the effects of dairy programs on farm viability was based on ERS' Agricultural Resource Management System (ARMS) data (Morehart et al., 2000). The analysis of the impacts of cooperative efforts by States to manage minimum prices was carried out using the University of Wisconsin-Madison Dairy Sector Interregional Competition Model (Cox and Dabidia, 2003). Knutson et al. (2003) contributed the summary of studies of the effects of the Northeast Interstate Dairy Compact in "An Alternative Milk Pricing Approach." Contributors to "The Evolution of the Modern Dairy Industry" and "Public Policy in the Dairy Industry" included researchers from the Texas A&M University (Anderson et al., 2003; Knutson et al., 2003); the University of Wisconsin-Madison (Cropp, 2003); Clemson University (Harris, 2003); University of California, Davis (Balagtas and Sumner, unpublished); and ERS (Blayney and Miller, 2003). ERS personnel provided overall project coordination, established the guidelines for analyzing the dairy program effects by defining the scenarios for analyzing program effects, and produced the final synthesis report.

The complete studies underlying many of the analyses presented in this report may be found on the web site of the Cornell Program on Dairy Markets and Policy (http://www.dairy.cornell.edu/CPDMP/Pages/Work-shops/Memphis03/), and on the ERS web site (Price, 2004; http://www.ers.usda.gov/publications/tb-1910).

The Evolution of the Modern Dairy Industry

Understanding the current state of the U.S. dairy industry and how it has changed over time is fundamental to a comprehensive economic evaluation of policy effects on the industry. This chapter examines changing demand for dairy products; changes in dairy processing, manufacturing, milk assembly, and distribution; structural change at the farm level; and changes in public policy—and identifies the forces underlying these changes.

Consolidation has changed the structure at all levels of the dairy industry— fluid processing, product manufacturing, producer cooperatives, and at the farm level. Advances in transportation, distribution, communication, and information technology have continued to expand the scope of dairy markets, lead to greater market integration, and change the nature of dairy markets from local markets for primarily fluid milk to national markets where manufacturing milk is dominant. These advances have allowed the market to be served by fewer, larger operations. Farm production systems have changed, new production systems have emerged, and production continues to be increasingly industrialized as labor is replaced with machinery and equipment. Productivity growth has allowed more milk to be produced with fewer cows, reduced production costs, and allowed producers to realize efficiencies from economies of scale. Dairy farms have become larger and more specialized in milk production, although there are still a large number of small dairy farms.

Changing consumer demand for dairy products has affected the structure of dairy farms. Slow growth in demand for dairy products, coupled with productivity growth, is driving this change. Since 1980, consumption of all dairy products has increased by 1.4 percent per year, while milk per cow has risen by an average of 2.1 percent per year (USDA, NASS). Fewer cows are needed to satisfy demand, but new dairy technologies require larger farms to justify the cost of adoption, resulting in fewer dairy farms (Cropp and Stephenson, 2001).

Regional shifts in milk production are a manifestation of some of the under-lying forces shaping the dairy industry. The growth of milk production in the Western United States and the emergence of large operations in this region have resulted in increased regional concentration of milk production, whereas farms remain more dispersed regionally. These shifts can have important impacts on the long-term prospects of milk producers in regions where production is declining.

Dairy policy has responded to structural change and the market conditions that give rise to this change as policymakers address problems that result from the effects of structural adjustment. National dairy policy has played, and continues to play, a role in the industry's evolution, but the impor-tance of policy as an agent of change is surpassed by the influence of these other factors.

At the same time, policy has been influenced by changes in the dairy sector. Institutions that comprise the U.S. dairy industry form an extensive and highly interrelated system, and changes in any or all of these institutions can require change in individual dairy programs (Hamm, 1991). Even though many of the policies examined in this report have been in effect since the 1930s and 1940s, the programs designed to achieve the policy objectives have been substantially changed in response to changes in market conditions.

The Changing Demand for Dairy Products

Changes in the demand for milk and dairy products have contributed to the transformation of the dairy industry. Per capita consumption of dairy products in the aggregate has risen over the past 20 years, while trends vary among individual products—fluid milk consumption has declined and cheese consumption has increased (table 2.1). Rising incomes, demographic shifts, and changing preferences have contributed in varying ways to consumer demand for individual dairy products. For example, *fluid milk products*,[1] which were once the major use for milk, now represent 36 percent of milk utilization (fig. 2.1). Other products, especially cheese, are the primary source of demand for milk. The shift in consumption from perishable fluid milk toward more storable and easily transported manufactured dairy products has contributed to the development of an increasingly national market for milk.

[1] Note: terms in **bold italics** are defined in the glossary.

Total sales of fluid milk are now virtually the same as in the mid-1970s, while per capita consumption has declined. A number of factors have contributed to this decline, including a smaller share of children in the population, the increase in meals eaten away from home, children's greater control over their food consumption, and stronger and more diverse competition from other beverages, particularly carbonated soft drinks, fruit and high-energy drinks, and bottled water. The negative effect of income on milk consumption is due to the increase in meals away from home as incomes rise. Since most fluid milk is consumed at home, fluid milk consumption falls as consumers eat out more frequently.

As incomes continue to rise, per capita consumption of fluid milk is expected to decline further, while per capita consumption of cheese and yogurt is expected to increase (Lin et al., 2003). Population growth is projected to outpace growth in per capita consumption of other dairy products such that total consumption is expected to rise.

Cheese has become a key element of dairy demand, with per capita consumption increasing by 75 percent between 1980 and 2002. Rising family incomes, the increased use of cheese as an ingredient in cooking, and increased consumption of cheese-heavy ethnic foods (like Italian and Mexican) have all expanded cheese use. The greater diversity and availability of cheeses has also fueled increases in total sales.

Less than half of all cheese is now sold at retail as cheese, but it is a major ingredient in many other foods sold through restaurants and grocery stores. The shift from at-home food preparation to consumption of partially or fully prepared foods has benefited cheese sales. Pizza and similar products may account for as much as one-third of total cheese use, and have been among the most important contributors to overall demand for dairy products.

Table 2.1—Dairy products: per capita consumption, 1980-2003[1]

Pounds

Year	Fluid milk and cream[2]	Butter	Cheese			Evaporated and condensed milk			Frozen dairy products				Dry products				All products
			American	Other	Cottage	Canned, whole	Bulk, whole	Bulk and canned skim	Ice cream	Ice milk	Sherbet	Other frozen products[3]	Dry whole milk	Nonfat dry milk	Dry butter milk	Dry whey[4]	Milk equivalent, milkfat basis
1980	246	4.5	9.6	7.9	4.5	2.8	1.0	3.3	17.5	7.1	1.3	0.3	0.3	3.0	0.2	2.7	543
1981	242	4.2	10.2	8.0	4.3	2.9	1.2	3.2	17.4	7.0	1.3	0.6	0.4	2.1	0.2	2.7	541
1982	236	4.4	11.3	8.6	4.2	2.7	1.3	3.0	17.6	6.6	1.3	0.6	0.4	2.1	0.2	2.9	555
1983	236	4.9	11.6	8.9	4.1	2.7	1.1	3.2	18.1	6.9	1.3	0.6	0.4	2.2	0.2	3.1	573
1984	238	4.9	11.9	9.6	4.1	2.4	1.3	3.7	18.2	7.0	1.3	0.6	0.4	2.5	0.2	3.2	582
1985	241	4.9	12.2	10.4	4.1	2.2	1.4	3.8	18.1	6.9	1.3	1.3	0.4	2.3	0.2	3.5	594
1986	240	4.6	12.1	11.0	4.1	2.2	1.4	4.3	18.4	7.2	1.3	0.9	0.5	2.4	0.2	3.7	592
1987	237	4.7	12.4	11.7	3.9	2.2	1.5	4.2	18.4	7.4	1.3	1.0	0.5	2.5	0.2	3.6	601
1988	237	4.5	11.5	12.2	3.9	2.1	1.4	4.2	17.3	8.0	1.3	1.0	0.6	2.6	0.2	3.5	583
1989	237	4.4	11.0	12.8	3.6	2.0	1.1	4.7	16.1	8.4	1.3	2.8	0.5	2.1	0.2	3.5	564
1990	233	4.4	11.1	13.5	3.4	2.2	1.0	4.8	15.8	7.7	1.3	3.7	0.6	2.9	0.2	3.7	568
1991	232	4.3	11.0	13.9	3.3	2.0	1.1	5.0	16.3	7.4	1.2	4.3	0.4	2.6	0.2	3.6	564
1992	229	4.3	11.3	14.6	3.1	2.1	1.1	5.2	16.2	7.0	1.3	4.3	0.5	2.8	0.2	3.8	566
1993	224	4.6	11.3	14.7	2.9	1.9	1.1	5.1	16.0	6.9	1.3	5.0	0.4	2.4	0.2	3.8	569
1994	223	4.8	11.4	15.1	2.8	1.8	0.8	5.5	16.0	7.5	1.3	4.8	0.4	3.5	0.2	3.8	580
1995	221	4.4	11.7	15.2	2.7	1.5	0.8	4.5	15.5	7.4	1.3	4.8	0.4	3.4	0.2	3.3	576
1996	220	4.3	11.8	15.5	2.6	1.5	0.8	4.0	15.6	7.5	1.3	3.8	0.4	3.7	0.2	3.3	566
1997	216	4.1	11.8	15.7	2.6	1.7	0.8	3.9	16.1	7.8	1.3	3.2	0.4	3.3	0.2	3.2	567
1998	213	4.4	11.9	15.9	2.7	1.4	0.6	4.1	16.3	8.1	1.3	3.4	0.4	3.2	0.2	3.3	572
1999	213	4.7	12.6	16.4	2.6	1.5	0.6	4.4	16.7	7.5	1.3	3.1	0.4	2.8	0.2	3.2	585
2000	210	4.5	12.7	17.1	2.6	1.5	0.5	3.8	16.6	7.3	1.2	2.9	0.3	2.6	0.2	3.8	593
2001	207	4.4	12.8	17.2	2.6	1.5	0.5	3.4	16.3	7.3	1.2	2.2	0.2	3.2	0.2	3.5	587
2002	206	4.4	12.8	17.6	2.6	1.8	0.5	3.7	16.4	6.5	1.3	2.1	0.2	3.1	0.2	3.4	586
2003[5]	204	4.5	12.7	17.9	2.7	1.9	0.5	3.1	17.4	6.7	1.3	2.0	0.2	3.4	0.2	3.4	594

Based on total population except for fluid products (resident population).
Product weight of beverage milks, fluid creams, egg nog, and yogurt.
Includes mellorine. May not be comparable across time.
Includes modified whey products.
Preliminary.

Source: ERS, from NASS data.

Figure 2.1
Milk utilization, 1975 and 2002
Billion lbs. milk

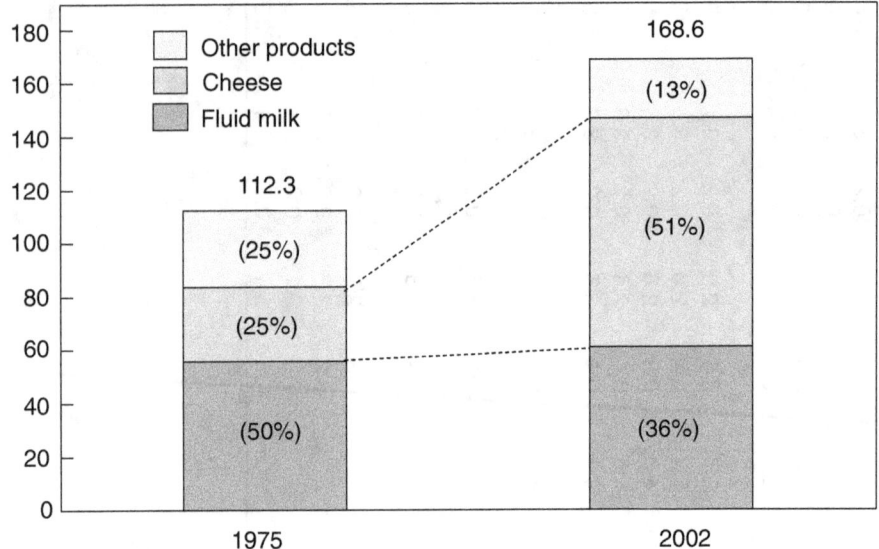

Source: ERS, from NASS, AMS data.

However, the rate of growth in cheese consumption appears to be slowing as the U.S. market approaches saturation.

Demand for quality-enhancing ingredients is expected to grow along with markets for pre-prepared foods. *Milkfat* and *skim solids* add flavor and functional quality to many processed foods. Dairy components like whey products and lactose have been a growth area in dairy demand, particularly as intermediate ingredients in foods. Demands for *milk-based fractions*, such as casein and whey proteins, and other dairy components have grown due to their desirable nutritional and functional characteristics and the logistical and cost advantages associated with storage and transport of dry products. New markets are expected to emerge for milk protein fractions with growing consumer and processor awareness of their benefits and increased demand for products that incorporate them.

Another important aspect of changing demand has been the shift in consumption from whole-fat to reduced- or low-fat milks and other dairy products (fig. 2.2). These changes are consistent with increased public concern about cholesterol, saturated fat, and calories. Increased consumption of reduced-fat milk has released butterfat that is used in ice cream and cheese production without producing a corresponding amount of *nonfat dry milk*. However, as cheese consumption has expanded, milkfat consumption has increased despite the shift in fluid milk consumption.

The prices of milk and dairy products, both own prices and prices relative to other food products, also influence consumption. The relationship between price and quantity demanded can be expressed numerically by the concept of an elasticity.[2] Estimates of the demand elasticity for all dairy products indicate that their demand is inelastic, or insensitive to price changes (table 2.2). When demand is inelastic, lower retail prices will result in a loss of industry revenue. This response is transmitted through the marketing chan-

[2]An elasticity expresses the percentage change in the quantity demanded of a product that results from a 1-percent change in its price. When quantity demanded changes by less than 1 percent, demand is considered to be relatively insensitive to price change, or "inelastic." If quantity demanded changes by more than 1 percent, then demand is responsive to price change, or "elastic." The elasticity measure allows the analyst to determine the expected impact of a price change on total revenue. If demand is inelastic, a 1-percent reduction in price will reduce total revenue (while a 1-percent increase in price will increase total revenue). Elastic demand would result in an increase in total revenue from a 1-percent price reduction (and a reduction in total revenue from a 1-percent price increase).

Figure 2.2
Consumption of beverage milk: whole fat and lower fat

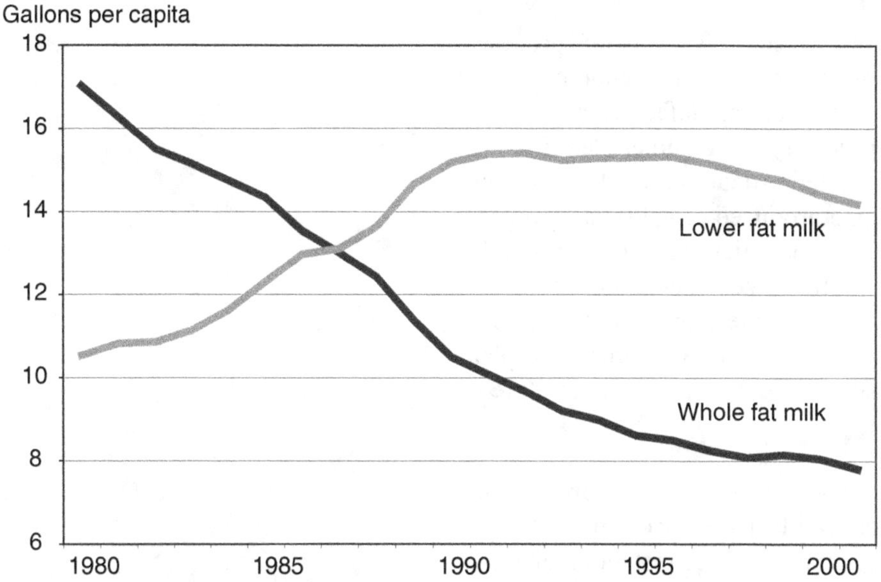

Gallons per capita

Source: USDA, ERS, Food Consumption Data System.

Table 2.2—Selected estimates of price elasticity of demand for dairy products

Product	Elasticity estimate (%)	Source
Fluid milk	-0.63	Heien and Wessels, 1988
	-0.076	Helmberger and Chen, 1994
Cheese	-0.52	Heien and Wessels, 1988
	-0.33	Huang, 1985
Butter	-0.73	Heien and Wessels, 1988
	-0.17	Huang, 1985

nels and ultimately affects producer returns. The empirical estimates of demand responsiveness suggest that dairy price reductions, whether they result from increased productivity or dairy policy actions, reduce aggregate producer returns.

Changes Beyond the Farmgate

The dairy sector is an interrelated and integrated market system in which changes in the structure and organization of one part of the sector affect the others. Developments in the processing, distribution, and assembly sectors—fluid milk *processors*, dairy product *manufacturers,* and producer *cooperatives*—are documented in order to explain the forces driving overall change in the dairy sector and the changing policy environment.

Dairy processing and manufacturing

Processing and manufacturing are considered as two separate subsectors. Processing refers to production of fluid milk products and manufacturing covers all the other dairy products. At every level of this sector, consolidation has resulted in fewer participants and larger unit size (whether the unit is a cooperative, a plant, or a firm). Structural change in this sector has been driven by both supply and demand factors.

Throughout the processing and manufacturing sector, fewer plants process fluid milk and manufacture dairy products. As advances in technologies associated with milk handling, storage, processing, manufacturing, and marketing have continued to create *economies of scale* and eroded dis economies, profit-seeking firms have expanded production facilities to take advantage. Plant size (measured by volume produced or sold) has grown considerably, providing evidence that scale economies are important in all segments of processing and manufacturing. Improved packaging, better coordination among storage and distribution activities, and transportation improvements have reduced the higher costs associated with increased plant size, such as higher distribution costs resulting from an industry structure of fewer and more centralized plants.

Developments in information technology have also improved coordination of product movement both within and between firms. Pressure from downstream businesses, including high-volume retailers, large restaurant chains, and food processors, have spurred dairy processors and manufacturers to grow large enough to serve customers efficiently; to satisfy requirements for more retail and other support activities, adoption of compatible technologies, improved product quality and uniformity, and production to firm-specific standards; as well as to offset *market power* of the large downstream entities (Kaufman, 2000; Blayney and Miller, 2003).

Structural change in processing and manufacturing has also been induced by supply changes. Despite advances in transport and other technologies that favor more centralized operations, many dairy processing and manufacturing firms still prefer to have an adequate, readily available local milk supply for plant operations. Farm milk production is geographically dispersed, and there are still cost advantages in producing perishable products close to consumers. Regional shifts in milk production have contributed to changes in the location of processing and manufacturing. As a result of the growth of milk supplies in Idaho, California, New Mexico, and Washington, butter, cheese, and nonfat dry milk production are increasingly located in the West.

Changes in consumer demand for dairy products have stimulated changes in product mix, structure, and organization. Fluid milk processing has been affected by changing demand for fluid products. Processors have struggled with changing fluid milk consumption, and have aggressively restructured in the face of sluggish fluid demand.[3] The number of fluid milk processing plants has declined continuously, while the average volume processed per plant has increased (fig. 2.3).[4] The number of firms has contracted as large proprietary fluid milk processing companies have consolidated through mergers and acquisitions. Over time, scale economies have been the major factor influencing consolidation of fluid processing plants, as the minimum efficient size continues to increase (Manchester and Blayney, 1997). New technologies in fluid processing raise costs, requiring a larger volume to cover costs. Fluid milk processing produces a homogenous product, with little opportunity for product differentiation, so lower costs are critical to the plant's ability to compete (Manchester and Blayney, 1997). In recent years,

[3]For more information on structural change in the processing and manufacturing sector, see Blayney and Miller, 2003; Miller, 2002; and Manchester and Blayney, 1997.

[4]This pattern of declining plant numbers and increasing plant size can be seen in all segments of the dairy processing and manufacturing sector. Similar figures for the other subsectors are not reproduced here, but can be found in Blayney and Miller, 2003.

Figure 2.3
Fluid milk plants and volume processed per plant, 1980-2001

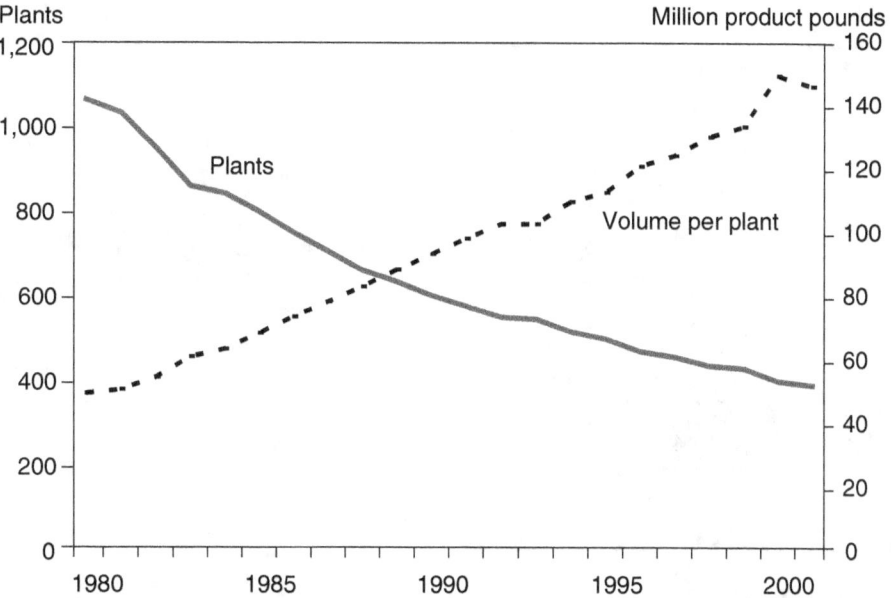

Source: USDA, AMS; Annual California Dairy Industry Statistics.

fluid milk processors have consolidated in response to consolidation at the retail level. The rise in supermarket mergers in the 1990s created incentives for fluid processors to consolidate to meet the demands of large retail accounts (U.S. GAO, 2001).

In contrast, firms that produce cheese and other products used in ethnic, prepared, and away-from-home food have benefited from the growth in demand for these products. Fueled by changes in eating habits, U.S. production of natural cheese has more than doubled since 1980, and has shifted from primarily American cheese varieties to other-than-American cheeses, like Italian varieties (fig. 2.4). Shifts in milk use from primarily fluid milk to primarily cheese have eased the constraints of distance, allowing product to be shipped greater distances and permitting greater centralization of manufacturing plants. Since 1980, the number of plants has fallen roughly by half. Combined with rising production, the average plant size has more than tripled (Blayney and Miller, 2003).

Demand for ingredients that are high in protein or have other nutritional or functional properties has expanded the market for dry products (e.g., nonfat dry milk, whey, and casein), assisted by the development of new technologies that allow milk to be fractionated into its most basic components. Manufacturers can isolate and use components with desired characteristics in other manufactured dairy products or in a variety of nondairy foods. Dry dairy products and components provide benefits to users by reducing byproducts or waste, reducing costs associated with perishability, and providing greater flexibility in plant location decisions (Stephenson, 2002).

Concentration measures have risen for nearly all segments of the dairy industry (table 2.3).[5] However, concentration rates are not as high as for other food processing industries, such as breakfast cereals and soybean processing, where the market share of the top four firms is in the 80-percent

[5]Fluid milk processing is primarily a local or regional industry, and much higher degrees of concentration characterize many local or regional markets (U.S. GAO, 2001). Also, the data in table 2.3 predate the 2001 merger of two large fluid milk processing companies, Dean Foods and Suiza Foods (Blayney and Miller, 2003).

Figure 2.4
U.S. consumption of natural cheese, 1980-2002

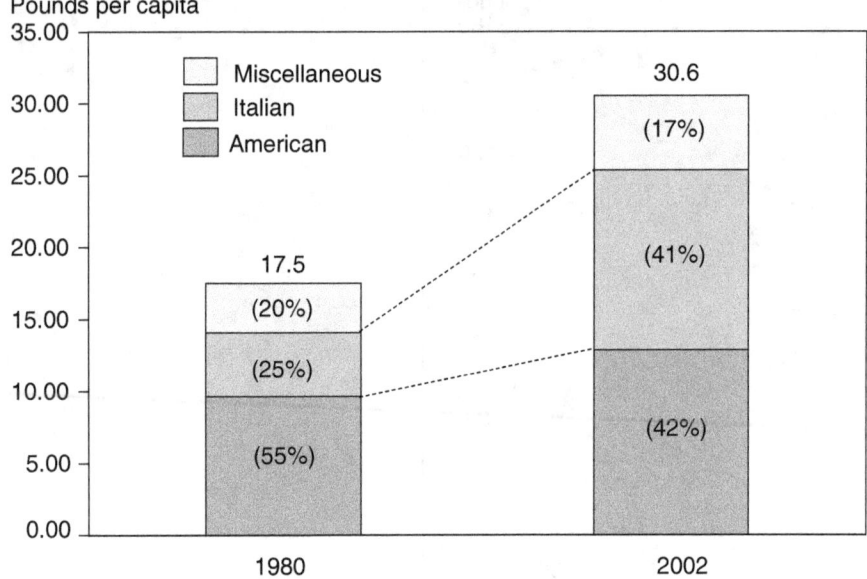

Pounds per capita

Source: ERS, from NASS data.

Table 2.3—Measures of concentration: market shares of largest U.S. dairy manufacturers/processors, 1963 and 1997[1]

Industry	Year	Share of total value of shipments of largest firms (%)			
		4 largest	8 largest	20 largest	50 largest
Creamery butter	1963	11	19	31	48
	1997	57	76	97	100
Cheese, natural	1963	44	51	59	69
and processed	1997	43	55	74	87
Dry, condensed, and	1963	40	53	71	90
evaporated dairy products	1997	69	78	87	96
Ice cream and	1963	37	48	64	74
frozen desserts	1997	39	54	76	90
Fluid milk	1963	23	30	40	48
	1997	23	35	52	73

[1]For data sources and methods, see Blayney and Miller, 2003.
Source: U.S. Department of Commerce, Economic Census.

range. Concentration among dairy processors and manufacturers and their customers has reduced the number of participants in the market and encouraged contracts or other forms of prearranged transactions. With fewer buyers and sellers, participants have begun to produce to custom—rather than standard—specifications, and are producing less of the commodity products that are traded on markets.[6]

Dairy product manufacturing occupies a key role from a policy perspective—American cheese, butter, and nonfat dry milk are purchased under the milk price support program (described in "Public Policy in the Dairy

[6]For more information on structural change in the processing and manufacturing sector, see Blayney and Miller, 2003; Miller, 2002; and Manchester and Blayney, 1997.

Industry"). The operations of processors and manufacturers, as they deal with both milk producers and dairy product consumers, are influenced by public dairy policies. For example, milk marketing orders affect the minimum price that manufacturers pay for fluid-grade milk used in manufacturing and that processors pay for milk used in fluid products. In some instances, milk processors' prices are higher than they would be in the absence of minimum pricing regulations.

Dairy cooperatives

Cooperatives play an important role in the dairy industry as intermediaries between member producers and their customers. Cooperatives are owned by producers, and one of their principal functions is providing members an assured market for their product. Some dairy cooperatives' sole function is marketing milk to fluid processors and dairy manufacturers and negotiating the best price for their members ("bargaining" cooperatives). Others perform many commercial functions, from milk assembly to milk processing and manufacturing of dairy products to distribution. Milk's perishability, the constant flow of the product, the lack of synchronization between demand and supply, and the inability to quickly adjust supply in response to demand changes creates the need for short-term balancing of supply and demand. Cooperatives have taken on much of the balancing function by coordinating assembly and distribution of milk from producer-members among the various users of milk and by processing it into *fluid products* or other products with longer shelf lives (like butter, nonfat dry milk, and cheese). In 2002, dairy cooperatives handled about 86 percent of farm marketings of milk, a share that has grown over time and is larger than shares of other commodity cooperatives (Kraenzle and Eversull, 2003; Ling, 2004).

There are considerably fewer dairy cooperatives now than 20 years ago, but they handle larger volumes of milk and serve wider geographic areas (table 2.4). Consolidation trends in the rest of the dairy industry have been a primary reason for consolidation among cooperatives (U.S. GAO, 2001). Consolidation among cooperatives usually followed consolidation among handlers or distributors, which had unbalanced the established power relationship. Consolidation allows cooperatives to integrate their operations in order to exploit economies of scale, more efficiently use manufacturing capacity, and reduce administrative overhead and transport costs (U.S. GAO, 2001). Dairy cooperatives are increasingly entering into strategic alliances, including joint ventures with proprietary firms, to ensure outlets for milk of their members.

A Federal law grants producer cooperatives limited exemptions from antitrust regulations, which allows them to use collective action to achieve and maintain market power. Thus, for example, cooperatives may be in a better position to bargain with processors for prices that are higher than

Table 2.4—Number of dairy cooperatives and market share, 1980-2002

Year	Number of dairy cooperatives	Farm-level share of farm marketings (%)
1980	435	77
2002	196	86

Source: USDA, Rural Business-Cooperative Service.

Federal-order minimum prices. These *over-order premiums* may be associated with quality and services and temporary changes in supply not considered in Federal-order minimum prices. Market power also derives from the fact that, although cooperatives do not regulate producer-members' milk production, they control the disposition of the milk supply. In addition, over-order premiums reflect short-term market conditions, which can generate prices that exceed minimum prices.

Dairy cooperatives' market power is closely tied to the treatment of cooperatives under *Federal milk marketing orders.* Federal-order minimum prices give cooperatives a basis from which to negotiate for over-order premiums (Cropp, 2003). Marketing orders allow cooperatives to vote on behalf of all their members (bloc voting). Because the initiative for a market order must come from producers, or from producers through cooperatives, bloc voting enables cooperatives to have considerable say in the establishment of an order (Manchester, 1983).

On the Farm—The Changing Structure of Dairy Farming

Dairy farming has undergone extensive structural change in the past two decades. Many of the changes that have taken place in the dairy sector are the result of market conditions (including those identified in the previous section), technological change, productivity growth, economies of scale, and regional shifts. Not all structural change is the result of policy, but these changes may result in adjustment costs that can become policy issues.

Dairy farming has several characteristics that distinguish it from other types of farming and complicate policy responses to dairy farm adjustment issues. Dairy farms have broad geographic distribution, reflecting the need to produce a bulky perishable product (fluid milk) near consumption centers. Much of the existing policy structure was initially developed to deal with these localized markets. As dairy markets have expanded, dairy programs have changed. For example, consolidation of Federal milk marketing orders, which resulted in fewer and larger orders, was undertaken to reflect the changing geographical boundaries of milk markets (USDA, RBS, 2002).

Dairy farming today is characterized by a multitude of production systems, each with different capital requirements and cost structures. Dairy farming has become a highly specialized type of agriculture, with specialized capital and high labor inputs. As a result, adjustment to change may be difficult because dairy farmers are less able to diversify as a strategy for managing risk. Dairy producers are also more dependent on farm income as a major contribution to household income than most other farmers, and are therefore less able to cushion the effects of adverse price movements with nonfarm income.

Structural change in dairy farming is of interest because of concerns about the economic and social effects of different production systems. As large industrial-style dairies have become increasingly important, concerns about environmental impacts have grown. The increased size of dairy farms and the declining share of smaller dairies have also raised concerns about competition in dairy markets and the viability of small farms. Because many of the largest dairies are in the West, where milk production is growing, shifts in competitiveness and measures to deal with their effects have become increasingly divisive regional issues.

Milk production: more milk from fewer cows

Driven by genetic and technological improvements, milk output per cow since 1980 has risen by nearly 50 percent and production has increased by nearly one-third, while cow numbers have declined (fig. 2.5). The number of dairy farms has declined by over 70 percent and the average size of dairy operations has increased, while the number of milk cows per farm has more than tripled (fig. 2.6). In 1980, over 60 percent of all dairy farms were in the smallest size class (1-29 cows). This share declined to less than 30 percent by 2002, while shares for larger operations increased (fig. 2.7). By 2002, dairy farms were more diverse in size, with farm numbers distributed

Figure 2.5
Milk production and cow numbers, 1980-2002

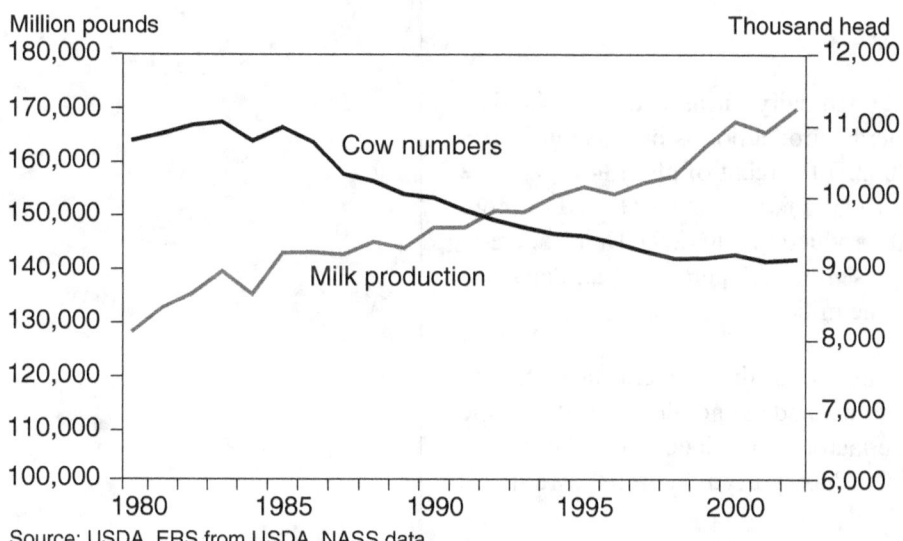

Source: USDA, ERS from USDA, NASS data.

Figure 2.6
Dairy farms and average cows per farm, 1980-2003

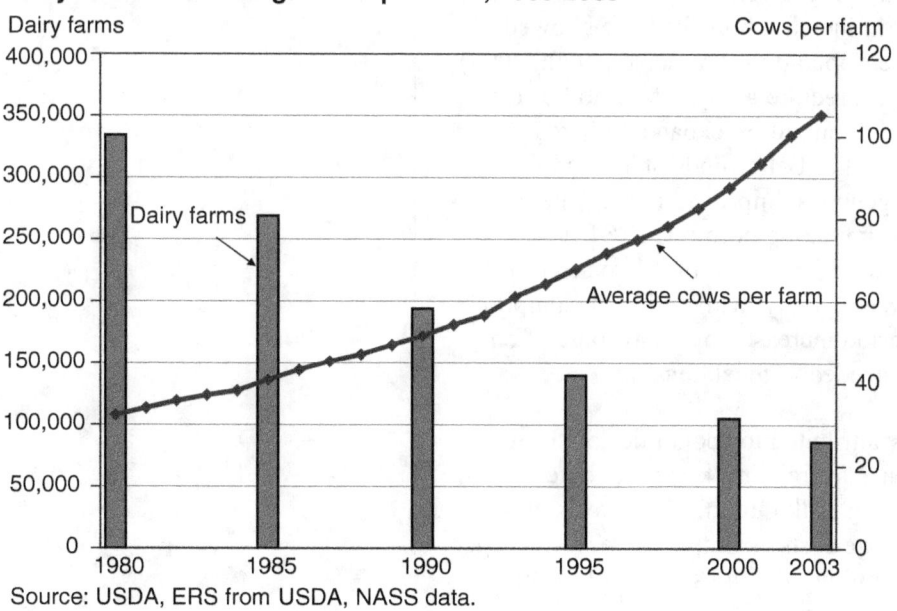

Source: USDA, ERS from USDA, NASS data.

Figure 2.7

Distribution of dairy operations by herd size, 1980-2002

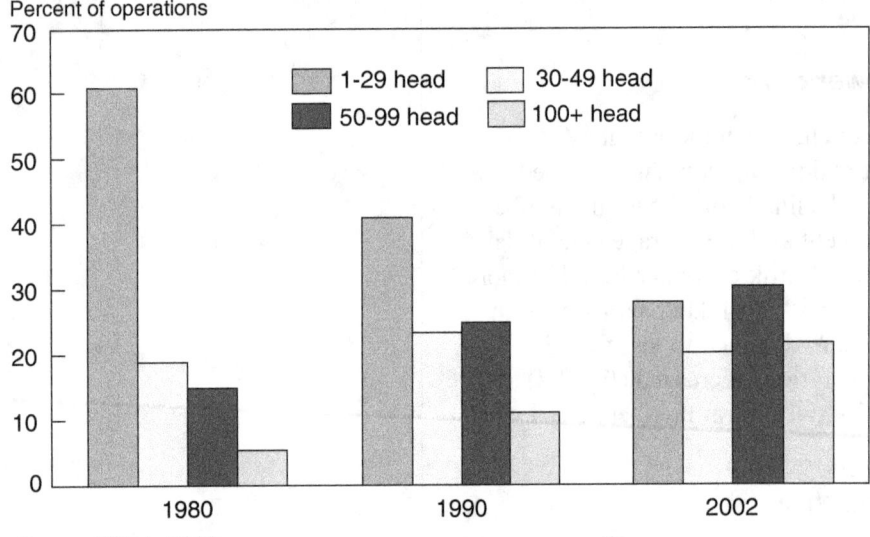

Percent of operations

Legend:
- 1-29 head
- 30-49 head
- 50-99 head
- 100+ head

Source: USDA, NASS.

more evenly across all size classes. Although dairy farms with small herds still outnumber farms with very large herds, production is increasingly concentrated on the largest farms. In 2002, 70 percent of all milk cows were on farms with 100 or more head (fig. 2.8), and farms with 200 head or more accounted for the greatest share of milk production (fig. 2.9). Dairy operations with 500 or more head, which represent only 3 percent of all dairy farms, now produce over 40 percent of the milk.

Changes in the structure of dairy farms are the result of several factors, but technological change, increased productivity, and economies of scale are the most important. The interaction of these factors, combined with relatively slow growth in demand for dairy products, has spurred the trend toward fewer and larger dairy farms.

Technological change over time allowed for increased production efficiency, the substitution of capital for labor, and reduced per unit production costs. Adoption of technologies that resulted in increased profits have allowed dairy farmers to increase the size of their operations (Anderson et al., 2003). At the same time, some new technologies require a larger farm to be cost effective. Dairy farmers can increase milk output by expanding herds, increasing milk production per cow, or both. Better understanding of animal health and nutrition, improved genetics, improved management practices, and treatments such as the milk-stimulating hormone rBST have helped increase milk production per cow. Since 1980, milk produced per cow has risen by an average of 2.1 percent yearly, while milk consumption (in all products) over the same time period increased by an average of only 1.4 percent—meaning fewer cows are needed to meet demand.

Average herd size growth is frequently attributed to economies of size or scale. Some producers are able to reduce average milk production costs, and thereby increase profits, by increasing milk output. Fixed milk production costs contribute to decreasing average costs as output increases. Larger operations may be able to use modern milking facilities more efficiently by

Figure 2.8
Distribution of milk cows by size of operation, 1980-2002

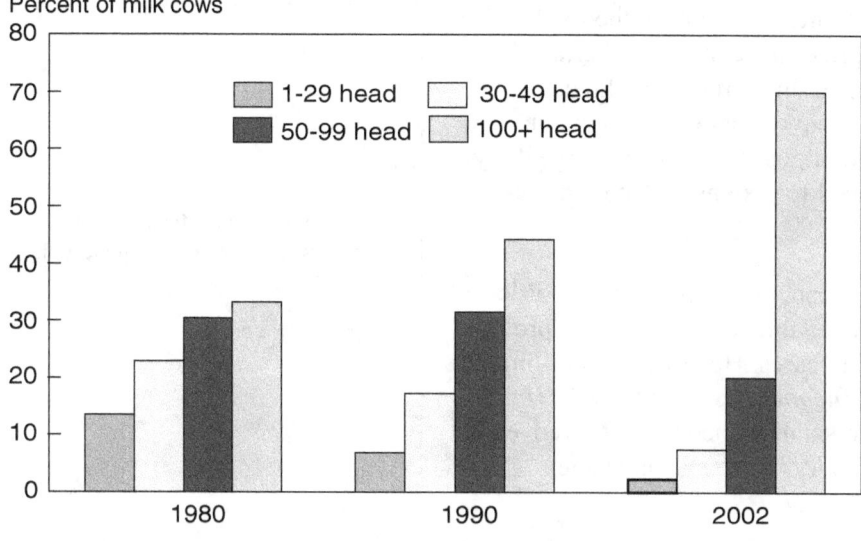

Source: USDA, NASS.

Figure 2.9
Distribution of milk production by farm size, 1993-2002

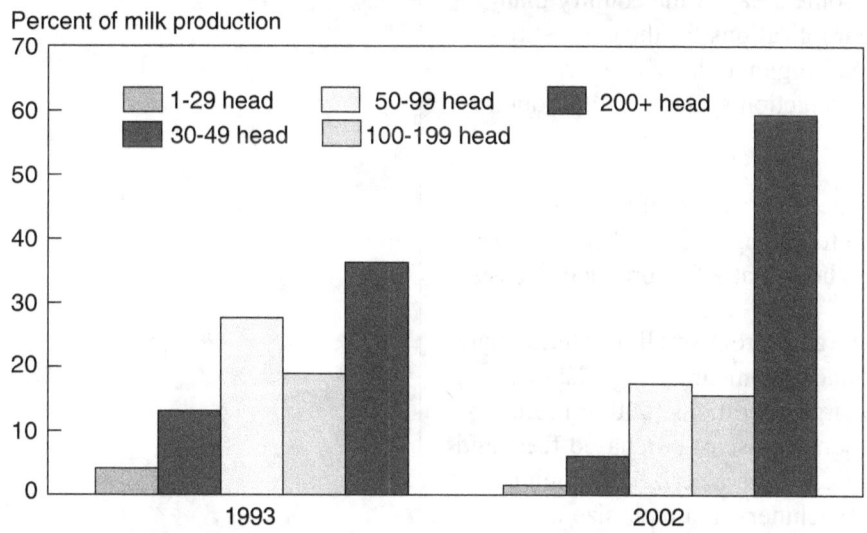

Source: USDA, NASS.

spreading the fixed costs of equipment over a larger number of cows
(Jackson-Smith and Barham, 2000). Volume discounts on purchased inputs
(such as feed) and on milk shipping charges, and volume premia paid to
large milk producers, may also contribute to economies of size. Technological advances in dairy facilities, equipment, and management practices have
reduced the diseconomies associated with larger herds, allowing producers
to expand. Empirical evidence supports a claim of decreasing average
production costs for milk (Matulich, 1978; Moschini, 1998).

Federal feed grain policy has been a force behind the rise of industrial-style
dairy farms and has contributed to the shift of dairy production to the West.
Federal grain policy has for many years subsidized feed grain production
and encouraged abundant feed grain supplies. With the availability of subsi-

dized feed grains, the dairy cow was altered from being a harvester of grasses and legumes grown on marginal crop land and in locations with marginal crop-growing weather into a consumer of energy in the form of grains. Since 1985, reductions in support prices have made feed grains less expensive due to Federal programs that increasingly relied on direct payments rather than price support and acreage restrictions to maintain grower returns. These changes helped make it possible to locate large dairy farms in hospitable climates without the need for extensive land requirements.[7]

[7]Hamm, Larry G., Michigan State University, personal communication.

The distributional effects of dairy programs can vary with farm size. Price supports without production limits, while available to all producers, provide more support as the size of the operation increases. However, output-limited payments like those provided by the *Milk Income Loss Contract (MILC)* program provide greater relative support to smaller operations. Moreover, as average herd sizes tend to vary by region, dairy programs may have different regional impacts.

Production systems may affect costs

Dairy farming is characterized by a variety of production systems. Some production systems are more adaptable to some areas of the country than others. Different production systems have implications for the competitiveness and longrun viability of dairy farms and regional dairy industries because of the close association between production systems and production costs.

Specialized dairy operations can be categorized in a variety of ways into a few basic types of production systems. The following is a broad characterization that focuses on feeding and housing methods that affect production costs.

- Confinement feeding systems may range from small to intermediate size operations, where feed is primarily homegrown and labor is supplied mostly by the family, to large operations (500 or more cows) with free-stall barns and extensive use of purchased feed and hired labor. Confinement operations are characterized by high capital requirements in buildings and machinery and their size may affect both costs and productivity.

- Pasture-based operations rely on grasses and other forages as the primary feed source. Pasture-based systems are characterized by reduced feed purchases, lower labor costs (cows harvest feed), and lower investment in machinery and buildings. A variant of this system, intensive rotational grazing, generally requires additional management skill involved with managing the pastures. Milk output per cow may be lower than in other production systems, but profit may be higher because of reduced costs.

- Dry-lot operations are relatively new, developing as dairying grew on a large scale in arid and semi-arid regions, particularly the West. Dry-lot systems generally feature a large number of cows, heavy use of purchased feed, and intensive, rather than extensive, use of land. They are among the lowest cost production systems because of low capital requirements and large size that allows for economies of size.

Each basic production system may vary according to the use of homegrown feed or purchased feed, the number of cows, the use of hired versus family labor, and other factors. Operations may also combine features of different production systems (e.g., part pasture, part confinement). The production system used will depend on climate; capital availability; availability of pasture, water, and land; costs of other inputs like feed and labor; and the producer's skill or preference.

It is impossible to make categorical statements about relative costs by type of production system—efficient, competitive farms can be found in each category. However, size matters. Larger operations benefit from the ability to spread capital costs over more units of production, and generally make more efficient use of inputs as the size of operation increases. Milk producers in the West have been found to have a significant cost advantage over producers in other regions because their operations are significantly larger (Short, 2004). Most dry-lot operations, which tend not only to be large but also have lower capital requirements, are located in the West, which may contribute to the West's lower unit costs.

In 2000, more Western dairy producers (50 percent) were able to cover total economic (operating and ownership) costs than operations in the upper Midwest and Northeast (30 percent each). An even smaller share (20 percent) of operations in the Corn Belt and Appalachia covered total economic costs in that year (Short, 2004). Declines in regional production shares have given rise to concerns about how to improve cost competitiveness in these regions (Eberle et al., 2003; Jesse, 2002; LaDue et al., 2003). Increasing herd size to reduce unit costs, adopting elements of lower cost production systems, or reducing input costs are some of the options considered.

Milk production growing in the West

Milk is produced in all 50 States and the top five in 2003 were California, Wisconsin, New York, Pennsylvania, and Idaho. These States now account for over half the Nation's milk output. The top 10 States accounted for 71 percent of all U.S. milk production in 2003 compared with 66 percent in 1980, indicating a slight increase in regional concentration of milk output. During that time period, New Mexico and Idaho—two of the fastest growing milk-producing States—replaced the Corn Belt's Ohio and Iowa in the list of the top 10 producing States. While the fastest growth in milk production has occurred in the West and Southwest, the Midwest and Northeast remain important milk-producing regions.

Despite the nationwide decline in dairy cows, a handful of States in the West and Southwest have added cows. Since 1980, the average herd size of dairy farms has risen several-fold in the Mountain, Pacific, Southeast, and Southern Plains and more modestly in the traditional dairy-producing regions (fig. 2.10). Traditional dairy-producing regions like the Lake States and the Northeast still account for high (but declining) shares of milk cows.

Most of the increase in aggregate U.S. milk production between 1980 and 2003 has been concentrated in the Mountain and Pacific States (fig. 2.11). These States' share of milk output doubled, from 19 percent in 1980 to 38 percent in 2002. Coupled with long-term milk output growth in California, strong growth in milk production in southern Idaho, eastern New Mexico, eastern Washington, and southwestern Kansas contributed to the growing importance of Western regions as major sources of milk supplies (Blayney, 2002-a).

Figure 2.10
Change in farm size by farm production region, 1980-2002

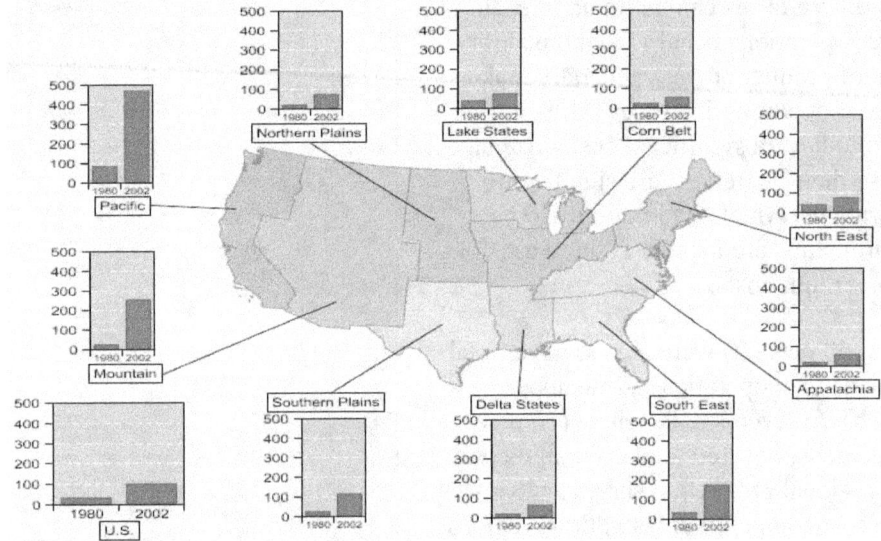

Note: Farm size is measured in average number of dairy cows per farm.
Source: USDA, ERS from USDA, NASS data.

Figure 2.11
Milk production shifts West

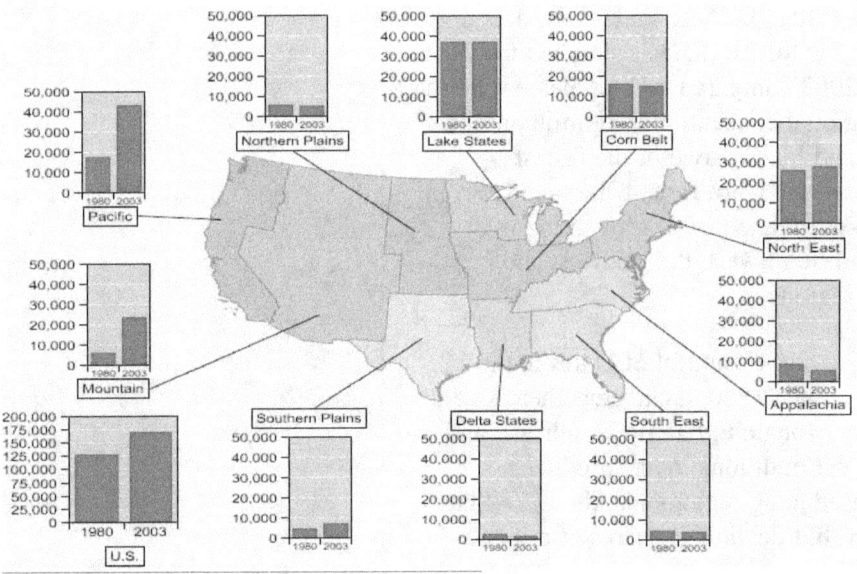

Note: Units are million pounds of milk.
Source: USDA, ERS from USDA, NASS data.

Although milk production and cows are increasingly located in the West, the greatest number of dairy farms continue to be in the traditional dairy-producing regions (Lake States, Northeast, and Corn Belt) (fig. 2.12). While all regions have lost dairy farms since 1980, the percentage decline in farm numbers was smallest in these traditional dairy-producing regions and highest in the Southeast, Delta, and Appalachia.

Several factors were responsible for the growth of dairy production in the West: less expensive land; lower production costs; favorable climate that permitted large-scale, dry-lot operations with lower costs; availability of production inputs other than land (including consistent and high-quality forage that allows for nutrient planning and certainty); access to hired labor; strong population growth that created demand for fluid milk and dairy products; and easy access to population centers that are markets for dairy products. (For a discussion of the factors that have influenced the growth of the dairy industry in California, see box, "California's Dairy Industry.") Production of milk for manufacturing use is increasingly located in the West and Southwest. As milk production there has grown, milk supply has exceeded fluid needs. Fluid utilization rates are relatively low—for example, 18 percent in California, 35 percent in New Mexico, and less than 10 percent in southern Idaho. Manufacturing plants base location decisions on proximity to milk supply rather than milk markets because their products are less perishable than fluid milk and easier to ship.

Figure 2.12
Dairy farm numbers decline throughout United States

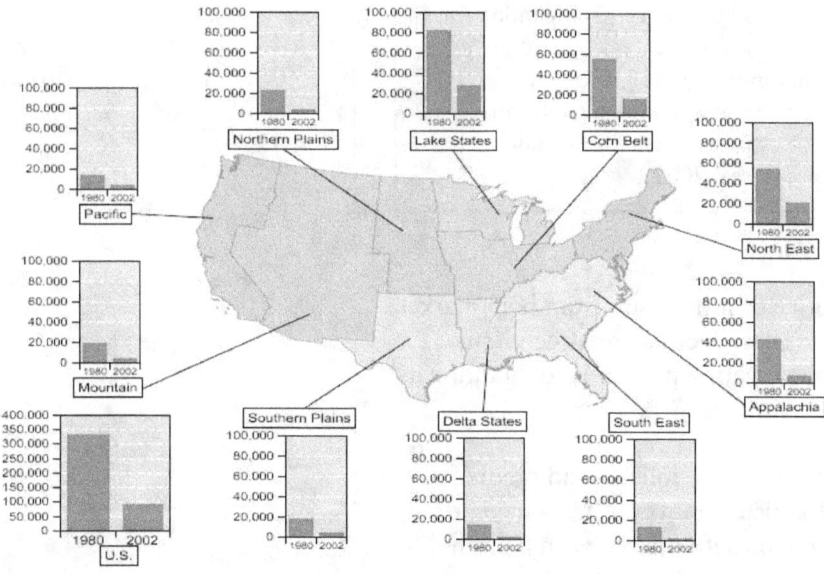

Source: USDA, ERS from USDA, NASS data.

California's Dairy Industry

California became the largest milk-producing state in 1993 and has continued to grow since. In 2003, it accounted for almost 21 percent of total U.S. milk production, and was also the largest producer of butter, nonfat dry milk, ice cream, cottage cheese, and whey protein concentrates. Cheese production is approaching that of the leading state, Wisconsin, and is projected to surpass it.

Climate, geography, natural resources, population, and technology have contributed to milk production and industry structure in California. An almost ideal climate provides a significant cost advantage relative to colder dairy-producing regions, and encourages large-scale intensive dairy operations with related economies of scale. The climate also favors the production of high-quality alfalfa as well as a large variety of crops whose byproducts are often cost-effective alternatives to conventional feeds. California milk production and milk and dairy product demand centers are geographically isolated relative to the rest of the United States, which has tended to constrain milk shipments into and out of the State. Thus, California has always had to assure itself of sufficient in-State fluid milk processing capacity. California's large and diverse population benefits the State's dairy industry by providing growing demand for dairy products and thus an impetus for industry growth. California's dairy industry has also benefited from early adoption of technology.

California suffers from irregularity of winter rain and snowpack that supply the water to the State's vast water storage and distribution system. Water is a crucial input for growing alfalfa, an important feed input to the dairy industry. Among crops that benefit from water subsidies, alfalfa receives the largest water subsidy, about $70 million (Kuminoff et al., 2000).

Several factors could significantly change the trajectory of California's dairy industry, notably water issues and environmental concerns. Competition for water supplies from a rapidly increasing population threatens agriculture's historic claims. Continued water availability in the future is likely a constraint on, rather than an advantage to, dairy production in California. Larger dairies, like those that are typical of California, tend to be more heavily targeted for environmental scrutiny (Jesse, 2002).

Changing economics of the dairy farm

Changes in farm income and the farm price of milk result from both market forces and changes in the dairy program. These factors are affecting the economics of milk production and may be creating pressures for additional change in the sector.

Farm income and profitability. Many agricultural policies and programs, including those for dairy, are designed to raise the level of farm income. ERS research has shown that as the economic activities of farm households have broadened, household income, household wealth, and other measures that focus on the farm household are better indicators of the well-being of farm families than the traditional farm income measure (Mishra et al., 2002). Between 1991 and 2001, dairy farm household income was slightly lower on average than the income of all farm households—$48,500 versus $51,000—and was close to average U.S. household income (data are from the Agricultural Resource Management Survey, or ARMS—see box, "Agricultural Resource Management System (ARMS) Data"). During this period, dairy farm household income ranged from 75 percent of the average income for all U.S. households in 1994 to 120 percent in 1999 and 2001.

Off-farm income, which includes earnings from off-farm employment, income from nonfarm businesses, pensions, and earnings from various household assets, has become more important to U.S. farm households for meeting household expenses (Mishra et al., 2002). Between 1991 and 2001, dairy farm households received a smaller share of their income—about one-third—from off-farm sources, compared with almost 90 percent for all farms. Larger dairy farms also receive a smaller share of household income from off-farm sources. If the trend toward larger dairy farms continues, off-farm income could comprise an even smaller share of dairy farm household income in the future.

Dairy farming is labor- and management-intensive, leaving less time for off-farm work than many other types of farming. In 1997, 79 percent of dairy farmers reported no off-farm work, compared with 42 percent of all farmers. Of those reporting any off-farm work, dairy farmers were much less likely than farmers in general (about 40 percent compared with nearly 70 percent) to work off-farm 200 or more days—essentially full-time.

In addition to income level, variability of farm household income and household wealth can affect the household's financial well-being. Owing to their dependence on farm income and the variation in dairy prices, dairy farm households experienced higher levels of income variation than the other types of farms studied (Mishra et al., 2002). The wealth (net worth) of dairy farm households was among the highest examined, but it is held mostly as illiquid farm assets, reflecting the large investment in specialized equipment.

Dairy farm households are less likely to have off-farm income to supplement returns from milk production, so profitability of the dairy enterprise is important. A long-term concept of profitability is defined as the difference

Table 2.5—Characteristics of dairy farms by economic cost group, 2001

| | Economic cost group [1] | | |
	Low-cost	Mid-cost	High-cost
	Percent		
Percent of farms	29	46	24
Percent of dairy value of production	61	34	5
Average number dairy cattle (number)	329	148	58
Herd size:			
Less than 100	25	47	88
100-299	52	46	NA
300-599	13	5	NA
600 or more	11	2	NA

[1]Low-cost farms have costs per revenue dollar less than 1; mid-cost farms' costs per revenue dollar are between 1 and 1.5; high-cost farms' costs per revenue dollar are greater than 1.5.
Note: Percentages may not add to 100 due to rounding.
NA: Not available due to lack of observations, an undefined statistic, or reliability concerns.
Source: USDA, Agricultural Resource Management Survey (ARMS), 2001.

between total economic costs and total revenue. Economic costs must be covered in order to sustain the farm business over the long run; they include total cash costs plus an allowance for depreciation as well as an imputed return to management and to unpaid labor of the farm operator and family (Morehart et al., 2000).

Table 2.5 compares total economic costs and total revenue and other farm characteristics for dairy farms, based on ARMS data. Revenue includes receipts from milk and dairy product sales and from sales of livestock, receipts from crop sales, government payments, and other farm-related income. The 2001 data include Dairy Market Loss Assistance payments but predate the MILC program.

The data can be used to evaluate the economic viability of dairy farms by measuring the revenue necessary to cover economic costs in a given year. Dairy farms are categorized as low-, mid-, or high-cost, according to their economic costs per dollar of revenue. Low-cost farms are defined as those that generate enough revenue to cover economic costs of production. In 2001, low-cost farms, while less than one-third of dairy farms, produced a disproportionately large share of dairy output measured by value (table 2.5). Mid-cost farms are close to becoming financially viable, and could achieve longrun economic viability with higher milk prices, lower production costs, and/or larger government payments. They accounted for the greatest share (46 percent) of all dairy farms in 2001, but proportionately less of the value of dairy production (34 percent). The high-cost farms represented the smallest share of dairy farms (24 percent), and a much smaller share of the value of dairy production (5 percent).[8] These farms require other sources of income or equity, such as retirement earnings or savings, to remain viable (Morehart et al., 2000). Survey data show that farms in the high-cost group have higher average off-farm earnings than either mid- or low-cost farms.

[8]Excluding the costs of imputed returns to unpaid labor increases the share of farms that are in the low-cost category.

The percentage of dairy farms that are financially viable can change from year to year, depending on the level of prices, costs, and government payments. For example, in 2000 (a low milk price year), less than 25 percent of dairy farms covered economic costs, while a slightly larger percentage fell into the mid- and low-cost groups than in 2001. This categorization does not predict the share of farms that will leave dairying. The data presented are for 1 year, and market and other factors can change over the course of several years. Also, many dairy farmers stay in business by supplementing farm revenue with off-farm revenue, or by accepting a low return for labor by themselves and other unpaid family members.

As structural change in the dairy sector produces a farm structure with fewer and larger operations, larger operations account for an increasing proportion of dairy farms and milk production. In 2001, dairy farms in the low-cost group had larger herd sizes, on average—over 300 cows per farm—while high-cost farms averaged fewer than 100 cows (table 2.5). Table 2.6 shows the breakout of each size class by economic cost group. Smaller farms tend to have a larger share of high-cost operations, while a higher share of larger farms are in the low-cost group. As the average farm size continues to increase over time, average dairy sector costs can be expected to decline (McElroy et al., 2002).

Milk price. Farm milk prices are influenced by a combination of market forces and dairy policy. Supply factors contributing to declining real milk prices include improvements in technology and management, increased milk per cow, slow growth in labor costs, and lower feed prices. On the demand side, growth in demand for milk and dairy products has been slower than output-increasing improvements, including milk yields per cow. Policy changes have also been a factor, including reductions in the milk price support level since 1980. The *all-milk price* has trended very slightly upward in nominal terms between 1980 and 2002, although it has declined in real terms.

Price variability is a concern for a number of reasons. Increased volatility adds challenges for farm business planning, debt repayment, and, in some cases, solvency. Variable prices contribute to price or market risk—uncertainty about the prices producers will receive for commodities. An important issue is whether the key concern is variation in prices or variation in incomes, cash flow, or net margins. These latter depend on both the price

Table 2.6—Economic cost categories of dairy farms by size class, 2001

Economic cost group[1]	Fewer than 100 cows	100-299 cows	300-599 cows	600 or more cows
		Percent		
Low cost	14	38	58	76
Mid cost	43	55	40	22
High cost	42	NA	NA	NA

[1]Low-cost farms have costs per revenue dollar less than 1; mid-cost farms' costs per revenue dollar are between 1 and 1.5; high-cost farms' costs per revenue dollar are greater than 1.5.
Note: Percentages may not add to 100 due to rounding.
NA: Not available due to lack of observations, an undefined statistic, or reliability concerns.
Source: USDA Agricultural Resource Management Survey (ARMS), 2001.

and the quantity of a product sold and the cost and amount of inputs used. For a dairy producer, variability in the milk price does not fully describe the variability in net farm income, because milk production costs and expenses also vary. These factors also need to be considered when understanding how variation in milk prices affects the dairy producer's bottom line.

Price variation arises from changes in supply and demand relationships. Variation in milk supply can arise from seasonality in milk production, variability in rainfall or other production conditions, input price variability (prices of feed, labor, or other inputs like electricity), and variability in producers' or processors' expectations of future prices. In the late 1980s, milk and dairy product prices became much more volatile than the previous two decades (fig. 2.13). Most analysts attribute this increased volatility to changes in the price support program—a lower price "floor" allowed greater downside price swings and reduced government stocks allowed greater price movements (Nicholson and Fiddaman, 2003). Other factors that contribute to increased price volatility include supply shocks (particularly from Western States) and a more inelastic demand for milk products due to rising incomes and increasing consumption of milk products in processed foods and meals away from home (Jackson-Smith and Barham, 2000).

Implications of changing farm structure

Change in the dairy farm sector over the past two decades has led to an increasingly diverse farm structure, with a variety of sizes, production systems, and cost structures. This diversity has complicated dairy program design, because dairy programs can have different distributional impacts by farm size and by cost structure. And, as farm size and production systems

Figure 2.13
U.S. all-milk, Class III, and support prices, 1980-2004

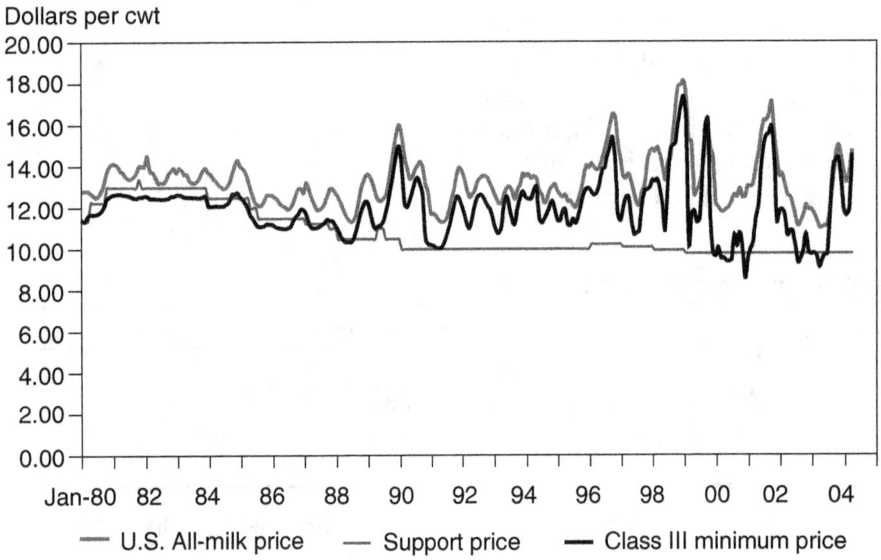

Dollars per cwt

Source: USDA, NASS, AMS, and FSA.

tend to vary by region, dairy programs can have different regional impacts. Increased diversity has created new policy challenges to address the effects of adjustment to changing market shares, new production patterns, and increased competition for a market that is growing more slowly than milk production capacity.

Conclusions

With per capita consumption flat or declining for almost all products except cheese, higher output at the farm level has led to lower real producer prices. Declining real prices have pressured dairy farmers to expand herds, adopt lower cost production systems, or exit dairying, leading to continued structural adjustment. Attempts to shelter dairy farmers from a set of diverse, powerful forces with a complex web of policies including price supports, import protection, regulated minimum pricing, and direct payments have done little to prevent structural change. The rate of structural change in the dairy sector is likely to accelerate as new technologies appear, and other factors (environmental regulation, land use, and contractual arrangements) continue the pressure for further consolidation and structural change (Anderson et al., 2003).

Public Policy in the Dairy Industry

"National dairy policy," as defined in the Congressional mandate, includes the following U.S. dairy programs:

- Federal milk marketing orders,
- the Federal milk price support program,
- State pricing programs and State mandated over-order premiums,[1]
- interstate dairy compacts,[2]
- direct payments to milk producers, and
- export programs such as the dairy export incentive program (DEIP).[3]

The above list is not exhaustive, and excludes import protection; supply management programs; demand enhancement programs; milk safety, sanitary, and environmental regulations; antitrust regulations (and limited exemptions); programs affecting input pricing and availability (like the feed grains program); and interactions with other commodity programs, among others. These programs are assumed to continue in their present form in order to isolate the effects of U.S. dairy policies identified in the mandate. Export credit programs, while a type of export program, are not evaluated because they are available for a range of commodities.

Policy or program objectives underlay a comprehensive evaluation of the economic effects of national dairy policy. Dairy program objectives, as stated in public documents such as authorizing legislation or mission statements of implementing agencies, are usually broad statements of purpose. Policy objectives may also be inferred from program provisions or operations. Generally, dairy policy seeks to enhance dairy producers' incomes, either directly through payments, or—more frequently—indirectly through price; and to maintain rural farm communities by promoting value-added agricultural activity (Hamm, 1991). Specific objectives vary according to each program, and include the support and stabilization of dairy farm incomes, ensuring stable and adequate supplies of milk and dairy products, providing stable marketing conditions for farm milk, and developing export markets for dairy products.

Table 3.1 presents an overview of the main U.S. dairy programs discussed in this report. Each program is related to its objectives, the main instruments used by each program, and the dairy products that each program targets directly.

Several existing dairy programs were originally designed to deal with the industry structures and economic failures of the 1930s. While the details of the programs have changed since then, their basic objectives and frameworks have remained largely the same. Seventy years ago, milk use was dominated by fluid consumption, markets were predominantly local, and many dairy enterprises were part of diversified farming operations. Today, consumption of cheese (rather than fluid milk) is the major use for milk, dairy product markets are increasingly national in scope, most dairy farms are highly specialized, and many are large-scale industrial operations. These

[1] The qualifier "State-mandated" has been added by the authors to distinguish over-order premiums regulated by State dairy programs from market-generated over-order premiums that are not part of any dairy program.

[2] Interstate dairy compacts are not part of current dairy programs.

[3] This chapter is intended to provide an overview only of the programs listed. For detailed information on program operations, the reader is referred to the web sites of the USDA program agencies, provided in the References.

Table 3.1—Overview of selected U.S. dairy programs

	Federal milk marketing orders	Milk price support program	State pricing, over-order premiums	Interstate dairy compacts	Milk Income Loss Contract (MILC)	Dairy Export Incentive Program (DEIP)	Other	
							Import measures	Promotion programs
Objectives:								
Stabilize market conditions	X	X						
Producer price support		X	X	X			X	
Producer income support	X		X	X	X			
Develop export markets						X		
Protect domestic programs							X	
Increase demand						X		X
Program instruments:								
Minimum price regulation	X		X	X				
Government purchase and storage		X						
Direct producer payments					X			
Export subsidies						X		
Tariffs, tariff-rate quotas							X	
Mandatory funding for product promotion, research, and development								X
Products:								
Milk	X		X	X	X		X	X
Butter		X				X	X	X
NFDM		X				X	X	X
Cheese		X				X	X	X
Other dairy products						X	X	X

Source: ERS, from various USDA sources.

changes raise doubts whether, after years of technological and structural change, existing policies still yield the same results as they did when they were conceived.

While U.S. policies and programs have played a role in shaping the structure of today's dairy industry, other driving forces including technological change—from the farm to the retail store—and changes in consumer demand have been even more important. Structural and technological changes have been important factors influencing policy change. Programs are modified when they are no longer relevant to the new market environment or to deal with the impacts of structural change at the farm level.

Appendix B shows a compressed history of public intervention in milk and dairy product markets, beginning with the 1930s. Even before the economic and social repercussions of the Depression triggered massive Federal government assistance to agriculture, State and local government agencies had experimented with dairy market interventions. Since the 1930s, Federal dairy programs have featured *parity pricing* and orderly marketing, measures to manage oversupply, and occasional introduction of more market-oriented program elements.

Early policy interventions were concerned primarily with providing equitable income for dairy farmers, as evidenced by policies focused on parity pricing and orderly marketing conditions.[4] Later dairy programs addressed chronic oversupply, including temporary use of voluntary *supply management* and, in the 1980s, linking the milk price support level to annual government purchases. Since 1985, dairy policies have been characterized by gradual introduction of greater, albeit still limited, market orientation through gradual reductions in the support price to a lower, "safety net" level. The pressure of Federal budget deficits led to the occasional use of producer assessments to help defray the costs of the dairy program. More recently, dairy policy has included ad hoc and countercyclical direct payments. Some recent programs target specific groups, such as smaller producers or producers in specific regions through compacts.

Since the 1930s, trade policy has supported domestic dairy programs through restrictive import policies—quotas that were replaced by tariff-rate quotas as a result of the WTO Agreement on Agriculture—and export subsidies (Blayney et al., 1995).[5]

Federal Milk Marketing Orders

Federal milk marketing orders (FMMO) establish minimum pricing rules for the sale of raw fluid-grade (Grade A) milk from the producer to the processor or manufacturer. Milk marketing orders were established in the Agricultural Marketing Agreement Act of 1937 (amended). In 1999-2003, between 65 and 76 percent of all milk marketed in the United States was marketed under FMMOs (USDA, AMS).[6]

FMMOs establish monthly minimum prices that first *handlers* of Grade A milk must pay, and verify that those handlers pay at least the minimum for milk delivered to them. The prices that producers actually receive may be

[4]According to Manchester (1983), orderly marketing arrangements sought to increase farmers' purchasing power by giving them market power through cooperatives.

[5]There are several sources of more detailed information on dairy policies, including Manchester, 1983; the Agricultural Marketing Service web site (http://www.ams.usda.gov/dairy/index.htm); the Farm ServiceAgency's web site (http://www.fsa.usda.gov); and the Foreign Agricultural Service web site (http://www.fas.usda.gov/excredits/deip.html).

[6]Including milk marketed under State marketing orders, the share of U.S. milk marketed under regulated pricing systems ranged between about 82 and 95 percent over the same time period. (For an example of a State system of marketing orders, see box, "California's Dairy Programs.")

higher, depending on market conditions. The differences between actual prices paid and the Federal order minimum price are called over-order payments, are market-generated, and paid outside of the order system.

A system of classified pricing establishes minimum prices for each end use—the fluid (class I) price is the highest, reflecting the higher cost of servicing the fluid market. Formulas relate the minimum prices for milk in each class to wholesale market prices for dairy products, which in turn are influenced by the milk price support program (fig. 3.1). The minimum price paid to producers is a blend price of all uses at the FMMO minimum Class prices (see box, "How Federal Milk Marketing Order Pricing Works").

Class I prices vary across the Federal milk order system. The Class I milk price is the higher of the Class III or IV price plus a location differential (*Class I differential*) specific to each pricing point in the country.[7] Regional differences among Class I differentials reflect the variation in the value of milk across regions. Class I differentials are set to encourage the movement of milk from milk-surplus areas into the milk-deficit areas (USDA, AMS, 1999). Despite that, substantial over-order premiums generated by the market are frequently needed to move milk to where it is needed to satisfy fluid demand.

[7]The Class I price differential is the amount added to a manufacturing milk price (the higher of the Class III or Class IV price) to derive the Class I milk price. It provides a minimum price that is reflective of the location value of milk.

Federal milk marketing orders were established during the 1930s to deal with the collapse of prices in milk markets and the seasonal loss of markets for many producers. FMMO evolved to address concerns that arise from the following characteristics of the milk market:

- raw milk is highly perishable;
- raw milk buyers are relatively concentrated compared with milk sellers;

Figure 3.1
Linkages between the milk price support program and the Federal Milk Marketing Orders

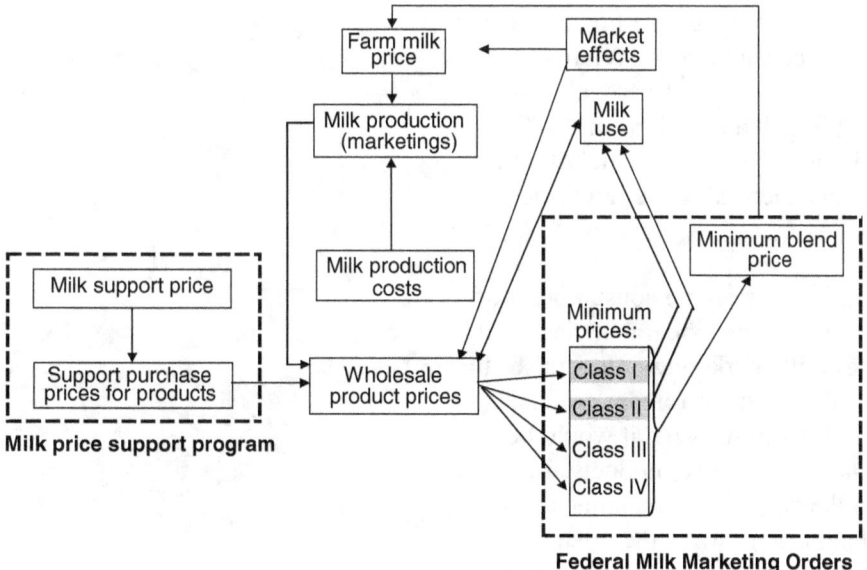

Source: Manchester and Blayney, 2001.

- fluid product and manufactured product demands are different, as are the costs of servicing those markets; and

- quantity of milk produced and quantity of milk demanded have different temporal patterns.

For example, Class I prices under Federal orders are set high enough to ensure that there will be sufficient supplies of perishable fluid milk to meet peak demand, while stabilizing the price to producers despite seasonal, weekly, or daily variability of production. In addition, requiring manufacturers and processors to pay minimum prices for milk was intended to balance the market power between producers and processors.

However, some of the characteristics of the milk market that gave rise to the order system were more prominent in the context of the technology and market structure of the early-to-mid twentieth century—advances in transportation and storage technologies, for example, have reduced (although not eliminated) marketing problems associated with perishability. Consolidation among dairy cooperatives and their increased share of milk marketings may have gone a long way toward redressing the imbalance in market power between milk sellers (producers, through cooperatives) and buyers (milk processors and dairy product manufacturers).[8] Cooperatives now bear more of the costs of coordinating and marketing milk from farm to plants. Other factors—like the disparity in timing between milk production and demand—still characterize dairy markets, although their impact on market flows is diminished. Because milk marketing orders—both Federal and State—have been in effect for so long, it is difficult to determine the extent to which these characteristics would emerge in the absence of FMMOs.

FMMOs are fundamentally aimed at equalizing competition between proprietary handlers and producers and promoting a greater degree of stability in marketing relationships.[9] Such a system effectively prevents a concentrated processing sector from exercising noncompetitive market power over milk producers by establishing minimum prices that all processors must pay for milk. Discriminatory pricing, to the extent that prices differ by more than the additional transportation and other costs entailed in meeting Class I demand, can increase revenue by charging a higher price in a market with more inelastic demand (where consumption is relatively unresponsive to price changes), and a lower price in a market with less inelastic (more price-responsive) demand (Tomek and Robinson, 1972; Manchester, 1983). Demand for fluid milk tends to be more inelastic than the demand for manufactured products. Thus, increasing the fluid price can increase total producer returns.

Milk marketing orders can have important impacts on the consumption of dairy products through their effects on prices. To the extent that classified pricing under the Federal (and some State) milk marketing orders raises the price of fluid milk and milk used in soft dairy products (cream products, cottage cheese, ice cream and related products) above what it would be in an unregulated market, the quantities demanded of these products are reduced. This increases the quantity of milk available for manufacturing uses (cheese, butter, and dried milk products), and lowers the price of Grade A milk used in manufacturing, increasing consumption of manufactured dairy products. Pooling milk revenues from all uses also provides

[8]However, the processing industry has further concentrated as well. See the discussion of concentration among cooperatives and processors in "The Evolution of the Modern Dairy Industry."

[9]For more information on how producer cooperatives interact with Federal milk marketing orders, see the discussion of dairy cooperatives in "The Evolution of the Modern Dairy Industry," and Cropp, 2003.

incentives for production of manufacturing milk—a dairy farmer producing mainly milk for manufacturing may receive a higher price because receipts from the sale of manufacturing milk are pooled with receipts from higher priced fluid milk sales (see box, "How Federal Milk Marketing Order Pricing Works," for an example of how revenue pooling works). This situation provides incentives for production of manufacturing milk and manufactured dairy products, resulting in lower prices and increased consumption.

In the Federal Agriculture Improvement and Reform Act of 1996, Congress mandated that the number of milk marketing orders be reduced and that several pricing issues be reexamined. The reform of the Federal milk marketing order system, effective January 1, 2000, reduced the number of Federal milk marketing orders from 31 to 11 to better reflect movements of milk, natural market boundaries, and existing institutional or market arrangements (USDA, AMS, 1999). It also made changes to pricing provisions, establishing a new Class I pricing structure, and established new minimum pricing formulas for Class II, III, and IV milk. The purpose of the pricing provision changes was to provide incentives for greater structural efficiencies in the assembly and shipment of milk for fluid milk products while maintaining equity among processors of fluid milk selling in marketing order areas and among dairy farmers supplying milk for fluid markets (USDA, AMS, 1999).

How Federal Milk Marketing Order Pricing Works

Two concepts form the core of Federal milk marketing orders: *classified pricing* and market-wide *revenue pooling*. Classified pricing means that milk is priced based on its end use or "class." Under revenue pooling, all producers selling milk under a particular milk marketing order share equitably in the market's revenue through a "uniform" or *"blend" price*, adjusted for location. Federal order minimum blend prices are the outcome of an accounting of how much milk is purchased by regulated handlers, and how that milk is used.

Classified pricing

Federal milk marketing orders establish minimum prices that regulated handlers must pay for *Grade A milk* [10] based on its use. The prices set are minimums—producers and/or their cooperatives are free to negotiate for prices above the minimum with the handlers buying their milk (Blayney et al., 1995). Market conditions and services provided by producers or their cooperatives can and often do lead to prices higher than the minimums.

There are four classes of milk under Federal orders; each class depends on how the milk is used:

Class I: Beverage (fluid) milk.

Class II: Fluid cream products, yogurt, perishable manufactured products (ice cream, cottage cheese, and others).

Class III: Cream cheese and hard manufactured cheese.

Class IV: Butter and milk in dried form.

Continued on page 42

[10]Grade A milk is milk that is produced under sanitary conditions that qualify it for fluid (beverage) consumption, although it may also be used to produce other products. Grade A is a quality designation, while the class price is based on how the milk is used.

All class (minimum) prices are set by formulas that reflect market conditions and prices are announced monthly by USDA's Agricultural Marketing Service. The highest minimum price is for Class I milk, recognizing the higher costs associated with supplying fluid milk markets.

The classified pricing formulas are based on the wholesale prices of dairy products that are purchased under the Milk Price Support Program (butter, nonfat dry milk (NFDM), cheese) and dry whey. Thus, if the wholesale prices of these products are being supported through purchases under the Milk Price Support Program, changes in the support price are reflected in the classified prices (fig. 3.1). The Class I price is determined by adding a location-specific differential to the price mover (the higher of the Class III or Class IV price), a price that reflects average wholesale market prices for manufactured prices (butter, nonfat dry milk (NFDM), and American cheese). The Class II price is determined by adding a differential to the Class IV price.

Revenue (price) pooling
Class prices are not paid directly to producers who deliver milk to the regulated handler. Milk receipts are pooled and a weighted average, or blend, price based on milk uses is paid to producers (including producer cooperatives) each month.

A simplified example based on a hypothetical order illustrates the procedure. In the marketing order covering the area surrounding Emerald City, four regulated

handlers are pooled under the order: a fluid milk bottler, an ice cream plant, a cheese plant, and a butter plant. Each handler is representative of one of the four class uses described above. Four farmers sell milk to each of the handlers, and all milk is Grade A.

Farmer	Sells milk to:	Class	Price[1]	Amount sold (hundredweight)	Receipts	Minimum blend price
Brown	Butter plant	IV	$10.89	37,000	$402,930	
Jones	Cheese plant	III	$11.41	80,000	$912,800	
Green	Ice cream plant	II	$11.81	15,000	$177,150	
McDonald	Fluid milk bottler	I	$13.96	48,000	$670,080	
Total				180,000	$2,162,960	$12.02

[1]These hypothetical numbers are for illustrative purpose only and are not meant to reflect actual class prices in any location.

Even though the producers sold their milk to different types of plants, they will each receive the same (minimum) price for their milk. The monthly minimum blend price is calculated by multiplying the class prices by the amounts of milk used in each class (utilization rate) to determine the total receipts under the order. The total receipts are then divided by the total quantity of milk (180,000 hundredweight) sold to the regulated handlers to determine the minimum blend price ($12.02 per hundredweight) each producer receives for milk sold that month.

Producer blend prices also vary regionally due to differences in the location differential for Class I milk and due to differing utilization rates—a higher rate of utilization of fluid milk, for example, will result in a higher average price received by producers. Milk supply and demand conditions, and any additional services provided by the producers, such as quality, timely delivery, and seasonal accommodation, may generate premiums that are paid outside of the order system.

Federal Milk Price Support Program

The Federal milk price support program was first authorized by the Agricultural Adjustment Act of 1933. Permanent authority for milk price support was provided by the Agricultural Act of 1949. Under the 1949 Act, which is currently suspended, the Secretary of Agriculture is directed to support the price of manufacturing grade milk through *Commodity Credit Corporation (CCC)* purchases of manufactured dairy products (mainly butter, nonfat dry milk, and cheese) at between 75 and 90 percent of parity (a price based on the relationship between farm milk prices and prices of farm inputs in a base period). These purchase prices are set at levels that enable manufacturers of average efficiency to pay farmers the support price for milk.

Farmers can receive more or less than the support price, depending on supply and demand conditions and market competitiveness. Plant location, the type of product manufactured, the quantity of milk delivered, milk composition, local competition between users of milk supplies, and plant operating efficiency all play a role in determining the price individual dairy farmers receive for their milk (Blayney et al., 1995). The dairy price support program supports the price of all dairy products in the United States.

For the first several decades of the program, the milk support price was established to maintain parity pricing. In the 1980s, concern over burgeoning stocks and rising program costs led Congress to sever the link between the support price and parity and gradually lower the support price. In 1988-95, triggers related to quantities of products purchased were used to prompt changes in the price support level.

The Federal Agriculture Improvement and Reform Act of 1996 (the 1996 Act) included a schedule for eliminating the support purchase program and replacing it with a processor recourse loan program. In the late 1990s, responding to low dairy prices, Congress instituted emergency supplemental payments to dairy producers and extended the support price program annually. The 2002 Act authorizes the support purchase program at the fixed support level of $9.90 per hundredweight through 2007 (see box, "Adjustments in Dairy Product Purchase Prices"). While there has been very little change in the milk support price since 1990, overall it has declined over the last two decades.

Outlays for product purchases and associated costs under the dairy price support have been variable. Since the early-to-mid 1990s, expenditures related to purchases of butter and cheese have declined substantially, while expenditures on nonfat dry milk have risen (table 3.2). The decline in total expenditures under the dairy price support program reflects the reductions in the milk support price in the mid-to-late 1980s (see fig. 2.13 in "The Evolution of the Modern Dairy Industry"). Dairy product purchases were lower, on average, in the 1990s than in the previous decade, although purchases of NFDM have risen in the past several years (fig. 3.2).

Table 3.2—CCC gross outlays for dairy products under the Milk Price Support Program[1]

Fiscal year	Butter and butter products	Cheese	Nonfat dry milk	Total
		Million $		
1980	343.3	482.8	554.2	1,380.3
1981	559.1	813.4	728.5	2,100.9
1982	600.4	941.9	883.5	2,425.7
1983	700.0	1,289.4	982.5	2,971.9
1984	479.5	1,043.8	790.6	2,313.9
1985	592.0	877.8	722.8	2,192.6
1986	701.0	879.2	844.0	2,424.1
1987	287.8	412.2	496.4	1,196.3
1988	544.3	458.8	337.3	1,340.5
1989	685.5	48.9	7.0	741.4
1990	456.4	1.2	23.6	481.2
1991	522.0	62.0	292.2	876.2
1992	568.7	2.9	30.1	601.8
1993	433.1	31.3	29.5	493.9
1994	279.2	0.2	112.2	391.7
1995	52.7	0.0	46.5	99.2
1996	0.4	0.0	19.2	19.7
1997	0.0	2.1	24.6	26.7
1998	0.0	0.2	166.3	166.5
1999	0.0	0.0	193.8	193.8
2000	0.0	8.2	487.6	495.9
2001	0.1	16.3	458.7	475.2
2002	0.0	6.2	610.7	617.0

[1]Includes outlays associated with purchases, storage & handling, transportation, processing and packaging, and other outlays. Exceeds total expenditures because sales proceeds, assessments, and other receipts are not included.
Source: USDA, FSA.

Figure 3.2
Purchases of dairy products under MPSP

Million lbs.

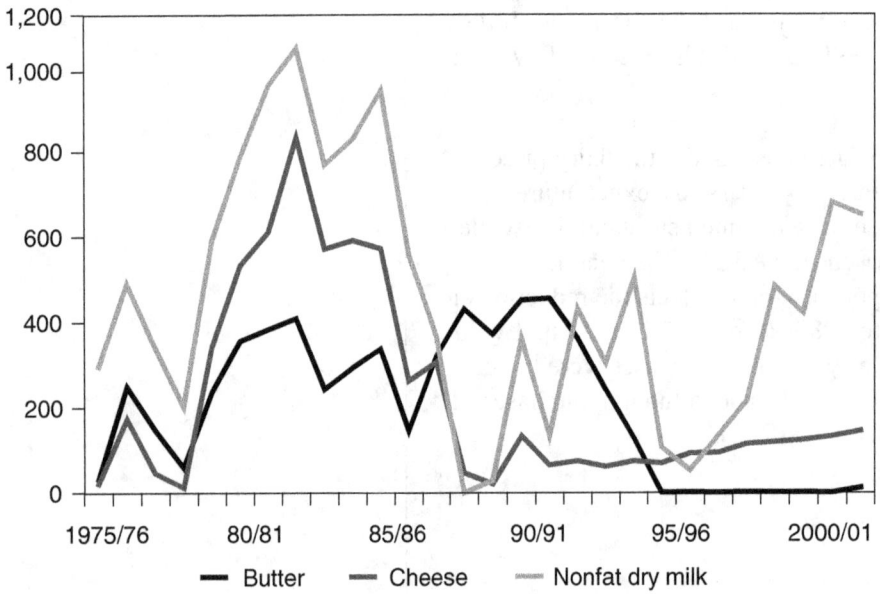

Source: USDA, FSA.

Adjustments in Dairy Product Purchase Prices

CCC purchase prices of cheese, butter and nonfat dry milk (NFDM) are set to enable plants of average efficiency to pay producers the support price for milk. A special provision for purchase prices of butter and NFDM allows USDA to allocate the rate of price support for milk between butter and nonfat dry milk by adjusting their purchase prices up to twice a year. Adjustments in purchase prices for these products should minimize Federal expenditures on the purchase of surplus dairy products, or meet other objectives established by the Secretary of Agriculture.

Unintended distortions can result if one of the purchase prices is set too high. For example, if the purchase price of NFDM is set too high, NFDM use and use of nonfat solids in products other than NFDM is reduced, and production of NFDM increases. The excess NFDM ends up as large CCC purchases. Because butter and NFDM are joint products, supporting the price of NFDM leads to increased production and a reduced price for butter, if the price of butter is above the support level.

The Secretary of Agriculture is authorized to adjust relative purchase prices of butter and NFDM twice during each calendar year. Because butter and NFDM are joint products, USDA may reduce the butter purchase price and offset the decline with an equivalent increase in the purchase price of NFDM without altering the underlying support price for milk (Salathe, 1993). The offsetting nature of these purchase price adjustments in the past few years is illustrated in figure 3.3. Adjustments in relative purchase prices of these products are colloquially referred to as the butter-powder "tilt."

The ability to adjust relative product purchase prices is important for correcting imbalances in the purchases of milkfat and nonfat solids. Failure to correct for such imbalances can create an incentive for producers to expand production and may alter the flow of milk to alternative uses. Food processors, who use significant amounts of milkfat and skim solids (the major components of butter and NFDM), are generally reluctant to change product formulations in response to price imbalances in the short run, but can be quite flexible in the longer term, further reducing the demand for the over-priced product.

Figure 3.3
CCC purchase prices of butter and NFDM, 1999/00-2002/03

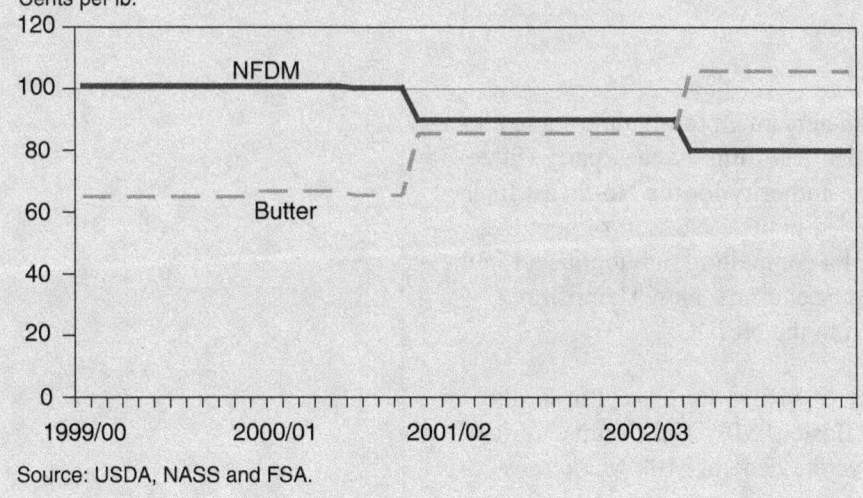

Source: USDA, NASS and FSA.

State Pricing and State-Mandated Over-Order Premiums

Individual States began to consider intervention in milk and dairy product markets during the Depression following legal constraints on Federal actions to regulate intrastate activity through marketing agreements (Manchester, 1983).[11] States focused first on price and income assistance for dairy farmers, but many extended their reach to both wholesale and retail milk and dairy product prices. State action to support fluid milk prices was economically feasible because fluid milk was the major use and fluid markets were primarily within State boundaries.

The number of State milk pricing programs has declined significantly—particularly since the 1960s—as interstate transportation of bulk and packaged milk made it more difficult for States to control in-State milk prices (Alexander et al., 1998). In 1998, Alexander et al. listed nine States with active State pricing or State-mandated over-order premium programs—California, Hawaii, Maine, Montana, Nevada, Western New York, North Dakota, Pennsylvania, and Virginia. California is the largest major milk-producing State that currently has an extensive state-level milk-pricing program (see box, "California's Dairy Programs").

States have used several methods to establish farm-level milk prices. Most States use regulatory authority to set minimum prices or mandate over-order premiums to be paid to producers above the Federal or State class price. These programs usually adopted the minimum Class I price in a nearby Federal order as the starting point for establishing the in-State Class I price. Some States then added a mandated over-order premium to the Federal Class I price to arrive at the State Class I price. These prices are, like Federal order prices, only minimums. For States, it is easier to control milk prices for fluid use because fluid markets tend to be more local in character.

Increasing market integration across State lines makes it difficult for individual States to operate over-order pricing plans.[12] Today, Pennsylvania is the only major dairy-producing State with over-order pricing. In addition, Pennsylvania uses wholesale and retail price control to prevent processors from undercutting Pennsylvania prices with lower-priced milk from other States (Alexander et al., 1998).

Interstate Dairy Compacts

A compact between or among States is an agreement to regulate some area of commerce that must be approved in identical form by each party (State) and authorized by the U.S. Congress. The authority for the Northeast Interstate Dairy Compact (NEIDC) was included in the 1996 Act, subject to a finding by the Secretary of Agriculture of a compelling public interest in the Compact region. Connecticut, Maine, Massachusetts, New Hampshire, Rhode Island and Vermont were included in the NEIDC.

The NEIDC established a minimum price of $16.94 for Class I milk, the milk used in fluid beverage products, in Boston, MA. The Compact price was generally, although not always, above the Federal Milk Marketing

[11]According to Manchester, "Since nearly all fluid milk markets were local in character and many were entirely within one State..., there was a question as to whether Federal marketing agreements...could be used. Early court decisions found that Federal regulation of purely intrastate markets was not legal."

[12]"An Alternative Milk Pricing Approach" discusses some of the issues involved in States operating over-order milk pricing programs through interstate compacts.

California's Dairy Programs

California does not participate in the Federal Milk Marketing Order system, but operates its own milk marketing order program with a classified pricing system (minimum prices for milk by end-use) and, since 1969, revenue pooling. Two differences between the Federal and California programs are the class structure of the pricing system and the calculation of producer prices through the pooling system. In addition, State fluid milk product standards affect milk production, processing, and marketing.

The producer milk price in California is priced based on five end-use classes, as opposed to four in Federal orders. Similar to the Federal marketing order system, pricing formulas relate class prices to milk components (fat and *solids-not-fat*). The California Department of Food and Agriculture announces minimum prices for specific uses. Revenue pooling depends on producers' quotas. Quota is allocated based on historical sales in Class I but can be freely traded among licensed California milk producers. Individual producers in California receive one price for quota milk and another price for nonquota milk.

In addition to a separate marketing program, California has unique standards for fat and solids content in fluid dairy products. The standards were part of a compromise in the early 1960s between producers and processors to pay producers for the fat and the solids-not-fat content of their milk. Milk containing 2-percent butterfat and 10-percent nonfat solids could be marketed if producers were compensated for the higher nonfat solids content of the milk. California standards for fluid milk have continued to evolve. Today, fortification is required in all fluid milk products in California.

California's fluid milk standards offer both advantages and disadvantages. They provide consumers with a more nutritional product, albeit at a higher price. The additional solids in California's fluid milk benefit dairy farmers in other States. The fortification requirement absorbs a large volume of nonfat solids that would otherwise be released onto the market, which could reduce the price of all U.S. milk if the nonfat dry milk price were above the purchase price, or increase Commodity Credit Corporation (CCC) purchases of NFDM. However, requiring that out-of-State milk meet the California standard may reduce competition and limit the availability of lower priced, although less nutritional, beverage milk products.

Order (FMMO) Class I price in Boston (see table 5.1 in "An Alternative Milk Pricing Approach"). If the FMMO Class I price was below the Compact Class I target price, processors were required to pay a Compact Premium into the Compact region's producer settlement pool, which was distributed back to eligible producers through a pooling mechanism.

The NEIDC operated from July 1997 to September 2001, but was not reauthorized in the 2002 Act. A discussion of the issues raised by the Compact and an analysis of the effects of such programs are the focus of "An Alternative Milk Pricing Approach."

Direct Payments

Although Federal farm programs for field crops (corn, wheat, etc.) began to shift from price support to direct payments beginning in the 1970s, direct payments played a minor role in U.S. dairy policy until the 2002 Act.

Dairy Market Loss Assistance (DMLA) programs in 1999, 2000, and 2001 provided funds for direct payments to milk producers to offset the effect of low prices. In each case, quantity limits were set on production eligible for payments. Direct payments were authorized in the 1980s but those payments were fundamentally different. Milk producers participating in two voluntary programs—the Milk Diversion Program and the Dairy Termination Program—had to reduce production or leave dairying to receive payments.

The Milk Income Loss Contract (MILC) program, established in the 2002 Act, provides monthly payments to participating producers when the reference price (FMMO Class I price at Boston) falls below the target price of $16.94 per cwt. The payment rate is calculated as 45 percent of the difference. An individual producer's total monthly payment is determined by multiplying the calculated payment rate by the amount of production eligible for payment. There is an annual quantity limit of 2.4 million pounds per producer on milk production eligible for payments. The quantity limit targets the program to smaller farms. Based on average yield in 2003, a farm with 128 cows would reach the production cap. Since Congress made the program retroactive to December 1, 2001, there is also a "transition" payment that covers the period from that date to the date the producer signs up for the program (signup began in August 2002 and continues until the program expires). The program is scheduled to terminate September 30, 2005.

Total payments under the MILC program since its inception, and payments to selected States, are shown in table 3.3. Because the program limits the quantity eligible for payments, States with a large number of smaller-sized operations (e.g., Wisconsin, New York, Pennsylvania, and Minnesota) receive a greater share of MILC payments than their share of milk production. States that tend to have large operations, like California, Idaho, Washington, and New Mexico, receive a small share of total MILC payments relative to their share of production.

Dairy Export Incentive Program

The *Dairy Export Incentive Program (DEIP)* was established in 1985. The DEIP "helps exporters of U.S. dairy products meet prevailing world prices for targeted dairy products and destinations" (USDA, FAS, 2003). Its major objective is to "develop export markets for dairy products where U.S. dairy products are not competitive because of the presence of subsidized exports from other countries" (USDA, FAS, 2003). Under the program, USDA pays cash bonuses to exporters, allowing them to export certain U.S. dairy products in targeted overseas markets. Commodities eligible for DEIP export are nonfat dry milk, butterfat, and cheeses. The program has been extended by all farm legislation since its inception, but since 1995 has been constrained

Table 3.3—MILC payments, top 10 and selected States

State	MILC payments, total to date[1]	State share of MILC payments	State share of milk production, 2002
	Thousand dollars	-------Percent-------	
Wisconsin	375,578	20.7	13.0
New York	170,185	9.4	7.2
Pennsylvania	164,164	9.1	6.3
Minnesota	148,533	8.2	5.0
California	123,476	6.8	20.6
Michigan	76,419	4.2	3.6
Ohio	69,893	3.9	2.6
Iowa	61,054	3.4	2.2
Vermont	40,914	2.3	1.6
Texas	38,914	2.1	3.1
Idaho	33,370	1.8	4.8
Washington	30,847	1.7	3.3
New Mexico	11,531	0.6	3.7
Total, all States	1,813,202		

[1]October 2002-January 2004.
Source: USDA, FSA.

by U.S. commitments under the World Trade Organization (WTO)'s Agreement on Agriculture. The quantities of product categories shipped under DEIP and the dollar value of awards since the beginning of the program are shown in table 3.4. Milk powder has accounted for the largest share of exports shipped under DEIP.

Other Dairy Programs

Import measures—protective tariffs and restrictive tariff-rate quotas (TRQs)—isolate the U.S. dairy sector from international markets, raise prices to producers, and prevent lower priced dairy products from compromising the price support program. Restrictive import policies for most dairy products reduce overall quantity demanded by keeping U.S. prices above world prices, but raise the quantity demanded of domestic dairy products by raising the price of imports to domestic consumers. Import protection, whether in the form of import quotas or high tariffs, was a necessary adjunct to the dairy price support program. Import policy supports domestic policy by maintaining high tariffs on most dairy products, preventing the unrestricted flow of lower priced substitute products from world markets. In the absence of border restrictions, lower priced products would enter the U.S. market, and CCC purchases at the higher support prices would rise to unsustainable levels. Further, with world prices well below CCC purchase prices for cheese, butter, and nonfat dry milk, the United States would have been directly supporting milk producers and taxpayers in exporting nations absent import restrictions. (For an illustration of the relationship between the domestic support programs and trade measures, see box, "Milk Protein Concentrates.")

Dairy promotion programs raise producer revenue by increasing demand for milk and dairy products. The Dairy and Tobacco Adjustment Act of 1983 authorized mandatory assessments on all U.S. dairy farmers and the Fluid

Table 3.4—DEIP quantities shipped and total commitments, 1987-2003

	Quantities				Commitments,[1] all products
Fiscal year	Butter and butteroil [2]	Cheese	Nonfat dry milk and whole milk powder	Total, all products	
	-- Tons --				$1,000
1987	0		287	287	289
1988	0		10,660	10,660	8,050
1989	0		0	0	0
1990	5,015		0	5,015	9,246
1991	11,070	2,000	17,400	30,470	39,261
1992	18,045	3,772	56,072	77,889	75,996
1993	14,149	4,205	168,243	186,597	161,797
1994	28,002	2,013	102,909	133,524	117,615
1995	38,550	3,425	204,261	246,236	140,225
1996	0	2,491	22,472	24,963	20,424
1997	18,003	3,650	117,216	138,869	121,462
1998	6,959	4,017	107,098	118,074	110,160
1999	395	2,779	133,148	136,322	145,308
2000	5,298	6,012	83,694	95,004	77,322
2001	0	3,030	55,451	58,481	8,488
2002	0	1,222	85,251	86,473	54,615
2003	10,000	2,272	73,883	86,155	31,526

[1]Total of bonus amounts committed for each commodity.
[2]Includes anhydrous milkfat.
Source: USDA, Foreign Agricultural Service.

Milk Promotion Act of 1990 authorized assessments on fluid milk processors. The assessments fund promotion (like the national "Got Milk?" advertising campaign) and research programs aimed at demonstrating or improving the nutritional or functional qualities of milk and dairy products (USDA, AMS, 2002). Several studies of the effects of generic promotion on dairy product markets and on dairy farm revenue have found that promotion efforts funded by mandatory checkoffs have been profitable for milk producers (Schmit and Kaiser, 2002; Chung and Kaiser, 2000).

Policy Conflicts

Because a number of dairy programs have been implemented over several decades—each with a different objective—it is inevitable that conflicts among programs arise. The price support program and the MILC program provide an example of problems that can be caused by conflicting policy outcomes. The price support program establishes a safety net floor under milk prices—milk prices are allowed to fall enough to induce a correction in oversupply or underconsumption. However, when the market price has fallen toward the price support safety net and thus is calling for an adjustment in supply, the results are partially muted by the MILC program, which, by providing production-linked funds to milk producers, may encourage production and retard the supply adjustment. The result is that milk prices stay lower longer than they otherwise would, increasing the likelihood of larger CCC purchases, and raising government costs for both programs.

"The Effects of National Dairy Programs" will examine the interaction between MILC and other dairy programs in more detail.

Regional Effects of Dairy Programs

Although most of the programs examined in this study are national in scope, many have effects that vary by region. The Milk Price Support Program supports dairy prices in the entire country, and the market-expanding benefits of DEIP benefit producers nationwide. Federal Milk Marketing Orders have different regional effects in those regions covered by orders. Class prices are based on the use of milk, and the blend price reflects the mix of uses in a region. Regions with low utilization of higher valued fluid milk will tend, other things equal, to have lower blend prices than regions with higher fluid utilization. Many of the fastest-growing milk-producing regions, like Idaho and New Mexico, tend to have low fluid utilization rates.

MILC, because of the limit on the quantity of milk eligible for payments, favors regions with large numbers of smaller farms. States with very large farms tend not to benefit as much from the MILC program, and may be disadvantaged by the program altogether due to the supply-inducing effects of MILC payments.

State pricing, State-mandated over-order premiums, and interstate dairy compacts may bolster dairy prices within the State or region covered by the program. The direct and indirect effects of interstate compacts will be examined in detail in "An Alternative Milk Pricing Approach."

Milk Protein Concentrates

Imports of milk protein products, including *milk protein concentrates* (MPCs), casein, and caseinates, highlight the interrelationship between trade policy and domestic dairy policy (Harris, 2003). While imports of casein have been an issue for over 20 years, the recent surge in MPC imports has driven the current debate.

MPCs and the U.S. Dairy Industry

In general, MPCs are processed milk products derived from skim milk. Development of ultra-filtration, which removes most of milk's fluid components and lactose while leaving a high concentration of milk protein, was largely responsible for the commercialization of this product (GAO, 2001).[13] Other forms of MPCs are manufactured by blending various products containing dairy proteins or manufactured through a precipitation process (Cessna, 2004). MPCs may contain from 40 percent to 90 percent protein and may be substituted for nonfat dry milk in some uses.

MPCs also have functional attributes that make them preferred for use in some products. For example, their low level of lactose enhances the efficiency of cheesemaking.[14] They are also commonly used in other foods, including frozen desserts, bakery products, and nutritional foods (high-protein sports drinks, energy bars, and nutrition supplements), and some nonfood uses (GAO, 2001). Because there is limited U.S. commercial production of MPC, and because these products enter the United States essentially duty-free, demand for the product is filled almost entirely by imports. Imports of MPCs increased rapidly in recent years, rising from 4,000 metric tons in 1989 to 65,000 metric tons in 2000, but have dropped off in recent years. In 2003, U.S. imports of MPCs amounted to over 48,000 metric tons (Cessna, 2004).

MPCs, Trade Policy, and Domestic Dairy Policy

The rise in U.S. MPC imports can be viewed as a secondary effect of U.S. agricultural and trade policy—the milk price support program and tariffs—and of technology and demand factors. The rapid rise in utilization and imports of MPCs has been the result of increased demand from the processed cheese industry, the U.S. nutritional foods industry and many other products that use MPCs, and low tariffs (GAO, 2001; U.S. International Trade Commission, 2004).

Trade policy is a major factor contributing to the rise in MPC imports. Under the World Trade Organization (WTO)'s Agreement on Agriculture, U.S. import quotas were converted to tariff-rate quotas (TRQs) with nominal within-quota tariffs that decline over time, and high over-quota tariffs. These over-quota tariffs have continued to insulate the U.S. dairy market. Prior to the WTO agreement, MPCs, in contrast to most other dairy products, were not covered by Section 22 quotas, and therefore were not subject to tariff-rate quotas under the WTO agreement (U.S. International Trade Commission, 2004).

MPCs were produced and traded in small quantities when the WTO agreement was negotiated, and consequently tariffs were low or nonexistent. The improvement of ultrafiltration technology allowed MPCs to be produced in

Continued on page 53

[13]The term MPC is used here to include both liquid ultra-filtered milk products and dry products.

[14]MPCs may be used in the production of nonstandardized cheese, or cheese for which FDA does not regulate ingredients through its standards of identity (GAO, 2001).

commercial quantities at reasonable cost, leading to an increase in quantity demanded of MPCs. MPC imports rose, taking advantage of the low tariffs. Under the WTO agreement, all agricultural tariffs are bound—once established, they cannot be raised without compensating the affected parties.

MPC use has also been encouraged by the high purchase price of nonfat dry milk (NFDM) under the dairy price support program that discouraged domestic production of MPCs and encouraged manufacturers to use other sources of protein, like MPCs.

The U.S. International Trade Commission found that the higher support purchase price for NFDM contributed to a higher return to processors on NFDM production than on production of MPCs, and concluded that the milk price support program created a disincentive to manufacture MPC in the United States (U.S. International Trade Commission, 2004).

The effects of MPC imports on government purchases and farm prices have been the subject of debate. Some analysts conclude that increased imports of MPCs have not only displaced some NFDM use in the United States, but have also resulted in an increase in government purchases over the past 5 years. The U.S. International Trade Commission estimated that imported milk proteins (including casein and caseinates) may have contributed about 25-35 percent to the growth in CCC stocks of NFDM during 1996-2002 (U.S. International Trade Commission, 2004), but that the effect on the farm price of milk was unclear. Bailey (2003) supports the hypothesis that MPC imports did not likely displace large amounts of domestically produced nonfat dry milk in cheese production during 2002 and concludes that any direct effect on farm milk prices would have been minimal.

Dairy farmer groups are concerned that MPC imports are displacing domestic milk used for cheesemaking and depressing farm milk prices. Some groups have urged the government to examine trade policy options for addressing MPC imports (Chite, 2001). Possible responses include proposed legislation to impose TRQs or quotas on imports and to provide Federal assistance to promote domestic MPC production.

The U.S. International Trade Commission (ITC) recently published the results of a fact-finding investigation on U.S. market conditions for milk protein products, focusing on MPCs, casein, and caseinate. For the full report see ftp://ftp.usitc.gov/pub/reports/studies/PUB3692.PDF.

For additional information see:

Bailey, Kenneth. *Impact of MPC Imports on 2002 U.S. Cheese Production.* Staff Paper 362. Dept. of Agricultural Economics and Rural Sociology, The Pennsylvania State University. March 2003.

Bailey, Kenneth. *Implications of Dairy Imports: The Case of Milk Protein Concentrates.* Staff Paper 353. Dept. of Agricultural Economics and Rural Sociology, The Pennsylvania State University. June 2002.

Bailey, Kenneth. *Imports of Milk Protein Concentrates: Assessing the Consequences.* Staff Paper 343. Dept. of Agricultural Economics and Rural Sociology, The Pennsylvania State University. November 2001.

Continued on page 54

Cessna, Jerry. *Milk Protein Products and Related Government Policy Issues*. USDA, Agricultural Marketing Service. February 2004.

Jesse, Ed. *U.S. Imports of Concentrated Milk Proteins: What We Know and Don't Know.* Market and Policy Briefing Paper 80. Dept. of Agricultural and Applied Economics, University of Wisconsin-Madison. February 2003.

U.S. General Accounting Office. *Dairy Products: Imports, Domestic Production, and Regulation of Ultra-filtered Milk.* March 2001.

U.S. International Trade Commission. *Conditions of Competition for Milk Protein Products in the U.S. Market.* Investigation No. 332-453, USITC Publication 3692. May 2004.

The Effects of National Dairy Programs

Introduction

Some of the dairy programs described in the previous chapter have been in place since the 1930s in the United States (see appendix B). Consequently, our understanding of their effects is limited because we have no observations of a "state of the industry" without programs.[1] Analysis of dairy programs' effects is therefore often based on counterfactual or, as used here, "modified" counterfactual approaches (see box, "Empirical Analysis of Dairy Programs Using Baseline Models"). For the purposes of this study, four national dairy programs are examined: Federal milk marketing orders (FMMOs), Federal milk price support, the direct payments to milk producers known as the Milk Income Loss Contract (MILC) program, and the Dairy Export Incentive Program (DEIP). These are only a subset of the programs that have been applied to the industry.[2]

Dairy Program Effects on National Market Indicators

The main focus of the results presented in this section is national, although we can, and do, report some effects for key milk-producing States. The methodological approach underlying the results is that the four national dairy programs are eliminated one at a time, and a simulation of industry indicators reflecting each removal is estimated. The final set of simulated industry indicators represents the cumulative effects of the program removals. In keeping with the mandate's objective to analyze the effects of programs, we compare the baseline simulation values to the final no-program estimates of the industry indicators. No changes in State-level programs are included, a potentially significant issue given California's position in the U.S. dairy economy (see box, "California's Dairy Programs" in "Public Policy in the Dairy Industry"). Nor are interstate dairy compacts considered given the "current policy" emphasis of the baseline models.

Two empirical modeling frameworks, FAPRI (University of Missouri) and FAPSIM (USDA, ERS) were used to estimate the effects of dairy programs (see box, "Empirical Analysis of Dairy Programs Using Baseline Models"). The two models are similar, but each offers advantages in terms of variables included, regional detail, and links to other analytical frameworks. Obtaining similar results from the two different frameworks provides analysts with greater confidence regarding the reliability of those results.

The empirical analysis exposes both the marginal effects of individual dairy programs and the cumulative effects of all the programs together. Further, the use of baseline frameworks provides year-by-year results. Strictly speaking, direct comparisons between the results derived from the two modeling frameworks are not appropriate—different baseline assumptions were used, a different order of program analysis was followed, and the averages are based on different time periods. The results are presented in terms of the effects of implementing programs—not eliminating programs. Thus,

[1]While we have no observations of the U.S. industry in the absence of extensive dairy programs, the experience of policy reform in other countries may provide some insights. Australia's deregulation of its dairy industry is described in an ABARE report on the impact of an open market in fluid milk supply at: http://abareonlineshop.com/product.asp?prodid=12204. The U.S. International Trade Commission has reviewed this report in *Conditions of Competition for Milk Protein Products in the U.S. Market,* Investigation No. 332-453, Publication 3692, May 2004. ftp://ftp.usitc.gov/pub/reports/studies/pub3692.pdf, p. 4-44 through 4-47.

[2]Two other elements of dairy policy were enumerated in the 2002 Act study mandate: State programs and over-order premiums; and interstate dairy compacts. Compacts are discussed in "An Alternative Milk Pricing Approach." We assume no changes in State programs since extensive State-level detail is lacking in the models underlying the analysis.

Empirical Analysis of Dairy Programs Using Baseline Models

The questions posed by the study of the dairy industry mandated in the 2002 Act are wide-ranging. No single model can provide the comprehensive analysis of the issues required by the Act. USDA marshaled, through cooperative agreements with Land-Grant University dairy economists, analytical capabilities available through existing modeling frameworks to address the questions. A major component of the analysis was utilization of "baseline models." Both the Food and Agricultural Policy Research Institute (FAPRI) and the Economic Research Service (ERS) of the USDA have devoted considerable resources to developing baselines for policy and program analysis. The FAPRI framework has a direct link to a farm-level analytical framework, FLIPSIM, housed at the Agricultural and Food Policy Center at Texas A&M University; the USDA model focuses on predominantly national questions.

The baseline models rely on a set of assumptions for a period of years into the future. For example, milk production responses to price changes are defined by fixed model parameters. Similarly, a set of parameters defines the demand side of the industry. The assumptions underlying the baseline values of dairy industry indicators are available at the following web sites: http://www.fapri.missouri.edu/Publications/2003Publications/BriefingBk03/03BriefingBk.pdf (FAPRI), and http://www.ers.usda.gov/publications/waob031/ (FAPSIM). Appendix C shows the baseline values for key dairy industry indicators used in the analyses.

The baseline models are developed in the context of existing programs. Baseline values reflect the assumption that current dairy programs are in operation. Program effects are then estimated mechanically, by deriving changes from baseline values in the absence of the programs. We hypothesized elimination of programs one at a time, an approach that uncovers both marginal and total effects, subject to underlying assumptions regarding program operations. No changes in border measures were made—the mandate emphasized domestic dairy program relationships as the priority.

Many analysts have noted that the annual basis for the baseline models can be problematic for program analysis. Baselines embody the best estimates of conditions that will exist in the context of program continuation and other factors such as normal weather patterns. Programs may be adjusted during the year. For example, the milk price support program may be altered by changing the combination of purchase prices for butter and nonfat dry milk known as the "tilt". Annual baseline models do not capture such a change unless it is built in from the beginning. More will be said on this point as needed.

The use of the baseline frameworks as described above is a modified counterfactual approach for determining dairy program effects. It is a modified approach because two simulations are used, one a baseline which includes program effects and the other a "without programs" alternative. A true counterfactual analysis generally rests on comparisons of estimated values of variables with actual values. Counterfactual approaches do not imply support or criticism of any particular policy—they are only a means of analyzing economic relationships under alternative hypothetical situations. It bears repeating that the study mandate does not call for an analysis of dairy program elimination. Elimination is only an artifice of the empirical analysis to derive program effects.

this study analyzes the effects of dairy programs and does not provide any recommendations regarding program elimination.

Table 4.1 shows the average effects of the package of four current dairy programs. The similar results from the two independent analyses suggest modest average program effects at the farm level (Brown, 2003; Price, 2004). With current dairy programs in place, the all-milk price is higher by about 1.5 percent and milk production and cow numbers are higher by 1.5-2 percent. Readers are cautioned again that these results are based **on a comparison of estimated baseline and hypothesized scenario results, not a comparison of estimates and actual values of data.** National dairy programs were found to raise producer cash receipts by about 3-4 percent.

National dairy programs result in higher nonfat dry milk (NFDM) and lower butter and cheese prices at the wholesale level. The combination of price support and Federal milk marketing order programs influences allocations of farm milk to final uses that contributes to the wholesale product price relationships. Higher milk production induced by higher milk prices

Table 4.1—National dairy program effects on industry indicators

Indicator/Variable	Contribution[1]	
	FAPRI[2]	FAPSIM[3]
	Percent	
Milk production	1.9	1.5
Milk cows	1.8	1.4
All-milk price	1.5	1.6
Producer cash receipts	3.8	3.4
Dairy product production:		
Butter	11.9	13.6
Cheese	0.7	0.3
Nonfat dry milk	31.8	28.0
Milk in fluid use	NA	-2.1
Dairy product prices:		
Wholesale		
Butter	-16.5	-21.3
Cheese	-2.8	-1.7
Nonfat dry milk	6.5	11.1
Class I milk price	NA	8.9
Retail		
Butter	-8.9	-9.4
Cheese	-1.8	-0.4
Fluid milk	7.7	3.4

[1]Effects as percentage (positive or negative) attributed to the four programs, relative to "No-policy" base, 5-year average.
[2]Food and Agricultural Policy Resarch Institute, University of Missouri
[3]Food and Agricultural Policy Simulator, USDA-ERS

Source: Brown (2003) and Price (2004).

results in greater availability of butterfat for both butter and cheese, resulting in lower prices for both products. We would expect fluid milk prices at wholesale to be higher due to classified pricing. The retail price effects are similar to those at the wholesale level, a reflection of the assumption that processors and dairy product manufacturers pass through input (milk or milk components) cost increases or reductions to consumers. Thus, consumers see lower butter and cheese prices and higher fluid milk prices than would appear in the absence of the programs.

As noted previously, the empirical analysis uncovers the marginal effects of individual dairy programs and a shorter run perspective since the baselines are established for a period of several future years (on an annual basis). The marginal effects of individual programs are tied directly to the order they are analyzed in each empirical model.[3] Why is this important? Consider the FAPRI model framework where the first program assumed to be eliminated is the MILC program. Since MILC is a direct payment program, it could partially offset any negative effects associated with the hypothesized elimination of one of the other programs first. When it is not available, the effects of the next hypothesized program elimination, milk price support in the FAPRI model, are unmasked. In the FAPSIM analysis, milk price support (CCC) is the first program to be hypothetically eliminated. Since MILC payments would still be made, they could mitigate milk price support elimination to some degree.

The marginal and shortrun program effects from the FAPRI and the FAPSIM analyses on milk production and the all-milk price are shown in tables 4.2 and 4.3. The interpretation of both tables is the same—a detailed discussion of the FAPRI model results illustrates how we can interpret these results. The starting point for the following discussion is the effect on the market indicators of the package of all four dairy programs. The 1.9-percent production effect and the 1.5-percent all-milk price effect in the far right column of table 4.2 correspond to the FAPRI model results shown in table 4.1. Additional information presented in table 4.2 includes estimates of the marginal contributions of each program to the cumulative average effects of all four programs. Year-by-year changes provide the shorter run measures of the effects.

In table 4.2, the average production effect of 1.9 percent has been disaggregated into four components, one for each dairy program. The operation of the Federal milk marketing orders contributed about 32 percent to the total percentage change, DEIP about 16 percent, the price support program about 21 percent, and the MILC program about 26 percent. The marginal effects of the programs for each year can be calculated as above. The annual effect on production from 2003 to 2007 attributed to all four programs ranges from 1.5 to 2.4 percent, with the larger impacts occurring early in the period. The earlier effects result from baseline modeling assumptions regarding production responses to the milk price changes associated with programs. The production adjusts to the changed prices over time so that effects of an initial change are diminished over time.

The average 1.5-percent all-milk price effect is decomposed in the same way, but the results highlight the countervailing effects of individual dairy

[3]The order of program removal followed in the FAPRI analysis was: MILC (first), price support (CCC), DEIP, FMMOs (last). The order for the FAPSIM analysis was: price support (CCC) (first), DEIP, MILC, FMMOs (last).

Table 4.2—Shortrun effects of selected dairy programs on dairy market indicators, FAPRI analysis

	2003	2004	2005	2006	2007	Average
Effects on milk production						
Scenario[1]			*Percent change*			
MILC	0.5	0.9	0.6	0.4	0.2	0.5
CCC	0.5	0.6	0.6	0.3	0.2	0.4
DEIP	0.0	0.0	0.3	0.5	0.5	0.3
FMMO	0.5	0.9	0.6	0.6	0.6	0.6
All selected programs	1.5	2.4	2.2	1.7	1.6	1.9
Effects on all-milk price						
MILC	-2.1	-2.9	-3.5	-1.8	-1.2	-2.3
CCC	3.4	3.8	-0.9	-0.9	-0.5	1.0
DEIP	0.0	0.0	2.2	1.7	1.3	1.0
FMMO	3.9	4.3	0.2	0.2	0.3	1.8
All selected programs	5.4	5.2	-2.1	-0.8	-0.2	1.5

[1] See text for scenario descriptions.
Source: Brown (2003).

programs. That is, the programs have both increasing and decreasing effects on the all-milk price. The argument that there is a basic incompatibility involved in operating both the price support program and the MILC program simultaneously is supported by these results. However, the two programs operate in fundamentally different ways. The milk price support program is designed to affect prices through markets for manufactured dairy products. MILC payments are made directly to individual milk producers. Without the MILC program, the remaining dairy programs raise the all-milk price by 3.8 percent over a 5-year period—when MILC is included, the increase is only 1.5 percent.

Annual estimates of all milk-price effects suggest there are significant underlying shortrun effects of dairy programs that must be recognized. For example, the effect of the milk price support program on the all-milk price is larger in the first year than in later years as milk supply adjustments take place. The differences in the annual baseline values of Commodity Credit Corporation butter, cheese, and nonfat dry milk (NFDM) price support purchases also play a significant role in determination of the price effects.

The FAPSIM results displayed in table 4.3 are interpreted in the same way. However, two aspects of the model are different from the FAPRI approach: the order of program elimination and the time frame for estimating longer term average effects. Since MILC is a direct payment program, its effects can offset negative effects associated with the elimination of other programs. Even with the differences described, the following similarities are seen: 1) the shortrun effects are greatest early in the time period of analysis, and 2) the offsetting all-milk price effects of the MILC and price support programs are present.

Table 4.3—Shortrun effects of selected dairy programs on dairy market indicators, FAPSIM analysis

	2002	2003	2004	2005	2006	2007	Average
Effects on milk production							
Scenario[1]			*Percent change*				
CCC	0.5	1.0	0.9	0.7	0.7	0.8	0.8
DEIP	0.3	0.5	0.5	0.5	0.5	0.5	0.4
MILC	0.2	0.4	0.4	0.3	0.3	0.2	0.3
FMMO	0.1	0.1	0.1	0.0	-0.1	-0.1	0.0
All selected programs	1.0	1.9	1.8	1.6	1.4	1.4	1.5
Effects on all-milk price							
CCC	6.0	7.4	-2.3	0.4	0.6	0.7	2.2
DEIP	4.6	0.4	0.5	0.5	0.3	0.3	1.1
MILC	-1.4	-3.0	-2.2	-1.5	-0.7	-0.4	-1.5
FMMO	0.9	-0.2	-0.3	-0.3	-0.4	-0.3	-0.1
All selected programs	10.1	4.6	-4.3	-1.0	-0.2	0.3	1.6

[1] See text for scenario descriptions.
Source: Price (2004).

As a general hypothesis, dairy programs would be expected to raise milk producer revenues, increase costs to consumers, and raise Government program costs. In table 4.4 the results of our empirical analysis in these three cases are shown. As noted previously, the results are conditioned by the model baseline values and the assumed milk supply adjustments over time. For example, if the underlying baseline exhibited high prices throughout the period of analysis, smaller or no impacts associated with the programs would appear.

Program implementations are estimated to add an average of about $1 billion annually to Federal Government outlays. These costs arise primarily from dairy product purchases for price support, payment of DEIP bonuses, and MILC payments. The costs relate directly to how programs are administered and whether program parameters are or are not changed (see box, "Adjustments in Dairy Product Purchase Prices" in "Public Policy in the Dairy Industry").

The annual average change in producer revenue ranges from about $1.2 billion to $1.9 billion. There are clearly much larger revenue (and Government cost) effects in the early years of the time periods being analyzed. A major factor in this "front-end" loading is the shortrun nature of the MILC program as originally implemented and its associated costs. As production adjustments to price changes implied by the models play out, the magnitudes of the effects diminish.

The estimates of changes in consumer expenditures on all foods are more divergent between the two empirical modeling frameworks, ranging from an annual average of about $1.8 billion to about $300 million. One reason

Table 4.4—Effects of dairy programs on producers, consumers, and Government expenditures

		2002	2003	2004	2005	2006	2007	Average
FAPRI results					Billion dollars			
Producer revenues[1]	Difference[4]		3.4	3.5	2.0	0.2	0.3	1.9
Consumer expenditures[2]	Difference[4]		2.8	2.9	0.9	1.2	1.2	1.8
Government expenditures[3]	Difference[4]		2.6	1.5	1.5	0.6	0.3	1.3
FAPSIM results								
Producer revenues[1]	Difference[4]	3.0	2.4	0.3	0.7	0.3	0.4	1.2
Consumer expenditures[2]	Difference[4]	1.8	0.8	-0.5	0.0	-0.1	0.1	0.3
Government expenditures[3]	Difference[4]	0.2	2.5	1.3	1.0	0.3	0.3	1.0

[1]Net revenue in FAPRI and gross receipts to milk producers in FAPSIM.
[2]Aggregate food expenditures in both FAPRI and FAPSIM.
[3]CCC net expenditures for dairy in both FAPRI and FAPSIM, fiscal year.
[4]Difference between "No programs" estimate and "Program in operation" estimate.
Source: Brown (2003) and Price (2004).

for the wide difference is likely the hypothesized effect related to FMMOs. Dairy economists generally agree that in the absence of the FMMOs there would still be a premium paid for milk going into fluid uses. The question is the size of the premium. A small premium would mean FMMO program effects are large. Large premiums imply smaller FMMO effects. The two baseline models reflect these hypotheses—FAPRI analysis assumes a $0.50 per hundredweight (cwt) premium while in the FAPSIM analysis the value is $1.30 per cwt. These results highlight the difficulties encountered in analyzing the demand side of dairy policy. Since dairy policies and programs are fundamentally producer-oriented, the consumer effects are indirect. Whether any change in dairy programs has large or small effects on consumers depends on consumer food purchase patterns, tastes and preferences for dairy products, ethnic background and other factors. Neither modeling framework employed in this analysis has a detailed demand component.

National Dairy Program Effects on Price Level and Volatility

Establishment of commodity price support programs is often tied to the objective of commodity price stability. Gardner (2002) suggests the link is not easy to uncover but that dairy price support has, at various times, stabilized milk prices. Since the late 1980s, milk and dairy product prices have become much more volatile, a situation that creates challenges for farm business planning, debt repayment, and in some cases, achieving or maintaining solvency. However, the milk price support program has put a floor under dairy product prices and the volatility can provide attractive buying and selling opportunities at low and high points in product price cycles.

Price volatility is examined using a system dynamics model developed at Cornell University (Nicholson and Fiddaman, 2003). The perspective taken for this component of the study is different from that taken in the previous section. Rather than comparing a simulation of program elimination with a baseline to provide estimates of program effects, this analysis uses simulations of changing dairy program parameters to generate estimates of effects on price variability. Table 4.5 summarizes MILC and milk price support program options and their effects on milk price variability. The FMMOs were also examined but the results are not shown here. They can be seen in Nicholson and Fiddaman (2003).

Programs influence both the level and variability of prices. MILC payments, which do not directly affect prices, have an indirect effect by increasing milk production. The MILC program results in lower all-milk and product prices, and lower price variation. Aggregate farm receipts (per cwt) are much less variable under the MILC program than in the base case due to the cushioning effect of direct payments.

Table 4.5—Measures of variability under selected alternative policy options

	Average[1]			Standard deviation[1]		
	Base	MILC[2]	Price support[3]	Base	MILC[2]	Price support[3]
Farm milk prices	*Dollar per cwt*			*Dollar per cwt*		
U.S. all-milk price	12.28	12.08	12.71	1.01	0.87	0.86
Farm receipts[4]	12.28	12.97	12.71	1.01	0.60	0.86
Wholesale product prices	*Cents per pound*			*Cents per pound*		
Cheese	121.51	120.07	125.23	9.41	8.41	7.42
Butter	113.35	112.35	116.02	13.58	12.85	11.98
Nonfat dry milk	86.51	85.12	92.60	11.71	9.65	9.85

[1] Average and standard deviation measured over 60-month simulation horizon.
[2] Implementing direct payments as per MILC.
[3] Raising milk support price by $1.00 from current $9.90 per cwt level.
[4] For the MILC policy option equals the all-milk price plus direct MILC payments.
Source: Nicholson and Fiddaman (2003).

Milk price support program effects depend on the level of support relative to market prices. Increasing the support price will increase average farm milk and product prices if it results in government purchases and stockholding. However, government stockholding is not a long-term solution—continual stock building with uncertain opportunities for disposal can become problematic. Increased support reduces volatility of farm milk prices, class prices, and dairy product prices. It would likely require very high support prices to completely eliminate price variation.

National Dairy Program Effects at the State Level

There is minimal subnational detail in the baseline frameworks underlying the analysis. The FAPRI model does include State-level production relationships on the supply side of the model. The effects of the selected dairy programs on key milk-producing States are not uniform (table 4.6). Because State pricing systems are unchanged, California producers are worse off when national programs are in place that promote increased production that pushes California class prices downward. Both the FMMO and California class prices are linked to dairy product market prices that tend to be lower when milk production is higher nationwide.

The all-milk price in all States reflects fluid milk prices and is linked to fluid utilization rates. The all-milk prices are higher with national programs in place, but key milk-producing States with less than 20-percent fluid utilization do not benefit as much as States with fluid utilization in excess of 35 percent (table 4.6).

Table 4.6—National dairy program's effect on all-milk price, selected States

	Baseline	Change from 5-year average "no programs" estimate	Fluid utilization rate[1]
	$ per cwt	Percent	Percent
Wisconsin	13.23	4.8	20.2
New York	13.61	9.5	41.6
Pennsylvania	14.63	9.2	42.4
Minnesota	13.25	4.1	20.2
Idaho	11.82	0.4	19.7
New Mexico	12.09	6.5	41.8
Michigan	12.98	6.2	36.9
Washington	12.53	0.6	27.0
Texas	13.42	8.0	41.8

[1]Utilization rates from appropriate Federal milk market orders in 2002.
Source: Brown (2003) and USDA, AMS, *Federal Milk Order Market Statistics, Annual Summary, 2002.*

The national dairy program effects on California's all-milk price were found to be negative (-3.4 percent). This apparently counterintuitive result is tied to the fact that no changes in the California milk pricing system were included in the model. Had California's system also been altered in response to Federal program effects, a positive change in the all-milk price would likely have occurred there. Moreover, we would expect market forces to generate premiums for milk in fluid uses that would at least partially offset the loss of fluid milk differential under FMMOs. Thus the effects in table 4.6 can be interpreted as maximum effects.

Effects of National Dairy Programs on Farms

An analysis based on a panel of dairy farms (table 4.7) suggests dairy programs improved the financial well-being of most, but not all, individual dairy farms (table 4.8). The results shown in table 4.8 show the total effect of the four individual dairy programs based on the results provided by the

Table 4.7—Selected characteristics of representative dairy farms, 2001

Panel farms State (region)	Financial condition with programs	Herd size	Milk per cow	Gross receipts per cow	Cropland	Annual milk production eligible for MILC payments[1]
		Number	Pounds	Dollars	Acres	Percent
CA	Good	1,700	23,500	2,829	800	6
NM	Marginal	2,000	21,400	2,879	400	6
WA	Good	185	24,600	3,648	120	53
WA	Poor	900	25,200	3,347	605	11
ID	Poor	750	24,000	3,081	240	13
ID	Good	2,100	23,500	2,933	560	5
TX (Northern)	Poor	2,400	20,100	2,651	260	5
TX (Central)	Poor	500	17,500	2,552	250	27
TX (Central)	Good	1,300	21,400	3,152	460	9
TX (Eastern)	Poor	330	15,000	2,230	600	48
TX (Eastern)	Good	750	18,700	2,793	750	17
MO	Poor	85	18,100	2,293	260	100
MO	Poor	400	20,000	2,201	730	30
FL (Northern)	Good	500	18,000	3,583	600	27
FL (Southern)	Poor	1,500	16,000	2,770	400	10
WI	Poor	135	23,500	3,423	600	76
WI	Marginal	700	22,600	3,077	1,200	15
NY (Western)	Poor	800	22,900	3,216	1,440	13
NY (Western)	Poor	1,200	22,500	3,176	2,160	9
NY (Central)	Good	110	23,700	3,771	296	92
NY (Central)	Good	500	23,200	3,340	1,100	21
VT	Good	134	22,000	3,307	220	81
VT	Poor	350	23,800	3,327	700	29
Panel average		840	21,357	3,025	641	33

[1]A maximum of 100 percent of any farm's production is eligible for payments.

Souce: Outlaw et al. (2003).

Table 4.8—Measuring dairy program effects at the farm level

Panel farms State (region)	Herd size	Effects of programs
	number	*dollars*
CA	1,700	-210,220
NM	2,000	365,280
WA	185	10,110
WA	900	-26,870
ID	750	-13,710
ID	2,100	-62,230
TX (Northern)	2,400	417,000
TX (Central)	500	97,140
TX (Central)	1,300	240,990
TX (Eastern)	330	66,570
TX (Eastern)	750	130,580
MO	85	26,200
MO	400	71,950
FL (Northern)	500	168,790
FL (Southern)	1,500	465,900
WI	135	13,620
WI	700	21,610
NY (Western)	800	179,080
NY (Western)	1,200	242,340
NY (Central)	110	38,010
NY (Central)	500	111,630
VT	134	42,050
VT	350	97,330
Panel average	840	108,398

Note: The values in the last column are interpreted as follows:
A positive value means dairy programs have a positive effect on net worth estimates.
A negative value implies programs depress the net worth estimates of the dairy.
Source: Outlaw et al. (2003).

analysis using the FAPRI analysis presented earlier (Brown, 2003). The change in longrun projected net worth over the 2003 to 2007 planning horizon is estimated for each panel farm.

The effects differ by size of operation (Outlaw et al., 2003). Programs have different effects on the individual farms for several reasons. MILC program effects depend on the share of production covered. The 2.4-million-pound cap on eligible production ranges from 5 percent of production on the largest dairies in the sample to well over 100 percent for the smallest. In no case may any producer receive payments on more than 2.4 million pounds of milk, but a producer well under the cap could increase production and receive added payments. The effects of the milk price support program and DEIP would be expected to be positive for all farms in the sample. Effects of the FMMO system, a fluid milk program, vary by location so that effects of classified pricing are unevenly distributed. The four large western U.S. farms that are less well off with programs (CA - 1,700 cows, WA - 900 cows, ID - 750 cows, and ID - 2,100 cows) is due in part to their location in areas of low Class I use. The results for the panel farms indicate that while some program changes might be necessary to keep the production sector of the dairy industry moving toward sound financial condition, not all producers benefit from or even desire such changes.

USDA's ARMS data (see box, "Agricultural Resource Management System (ARMS) Data" in "The Evolution of the Modern Dairy Industry") provides additional insight on the effects of national dairy programs on dairy farms and their long-term profitability.[4] Using the ARMS data, dairy farms can be divided into three groups according to their economic costs per dollar of revenue. Low-cost farms generate enough revenue to cover economic costs of production (costs per dollar of revenue are less than 1). In 2001, an estimated 29 percent of dairy farms were in the low-cost group and they produced 62 percent of dairy output measured by value. Mid-cost farms (those with costs per dollar of revenue between 1 and 1.5) are those close to becoming financially viable and could do so with higher milk prices, lower production costs, and/or larger government payments. They accounted for about 46 percent of all dairy farms in 2001, and 33 percent of the value of dairy production. The high-cost farms (costs per revenue dollar of 1.5 or higher) represented about 24 percent of dairy farms, but only 5 percent of the value of dairy production. These farms require other sources of income or equity, such as off-farm employment, retirement earnings, or savings to remain viable (Morehart et al., 2000). The data show that high-cost farms have higher average off-farm earnings than either mid- or low-cost farms.

One approach for assessing the viability of dairy farms in any given year is to measure the revenue necessary to cover long-term economic costs. The share of dairy farms that are financially viable can change from year to year, depending on the level of prices, costs, and government payments. For example, in 2000 (a low milk price year), less than 25 percent covered economic costs, allowing them to sustain the farm business over many years. A larger percentage fell into the mid- and low-cost groups than in 2001.

Government policy can affect farm viability through revenue impacts related to milk price (market receipts), and through direct government payments. While ARMS provides data on government payments, it is not possible to discern the influence of policy on price. The set of selected national dairy programs—the milk price support program, DEIP, and FMMOs—raises the all-milk price by an average 4 percent over a 5-year period. Because ARMS data do not include MILC payments, the effects of MILC on the all-milk price are excluded.

A static analysis based on 2001 data shows that higher milk prices resulting from national dairy programs improved the short- to medium-term profitability and viability of dairy producers. The share of dairy farms that would cover longrun economic costs increases from 24 to 29 percent (fig. 4.1), and the share of farms that require other sources of income or equity to remain viable declines from 26 to 24 percent. A targeted direct payment program like MILC will improve the viability of mid- and high-cost producers who have high percentages of their production eligible for payments. Lower cost producers will always be profitable in the long run, making it possible for them to expand production to gain market share.

[4]Long-term profitability is defined as the difference between economic costs and total revenue. Economic costs must be covered in order to sustain the farm business over the long run. They include total cash costs plus an allowance for depreciation as well as an imputed return to management and to unpaid labor of the farm operator and family (Morehart et al., 2000). Revenue includes receipts from milk and dairy product sales, government payments, and crop insurance indemnity payments. The 2001 ARMS data includes Dairy Market Loss Assistance payments but predates the MILC program.

Figure 4.1
**Effect of 4-percent milk price increase on dairy farm
cost distribution, 2001**

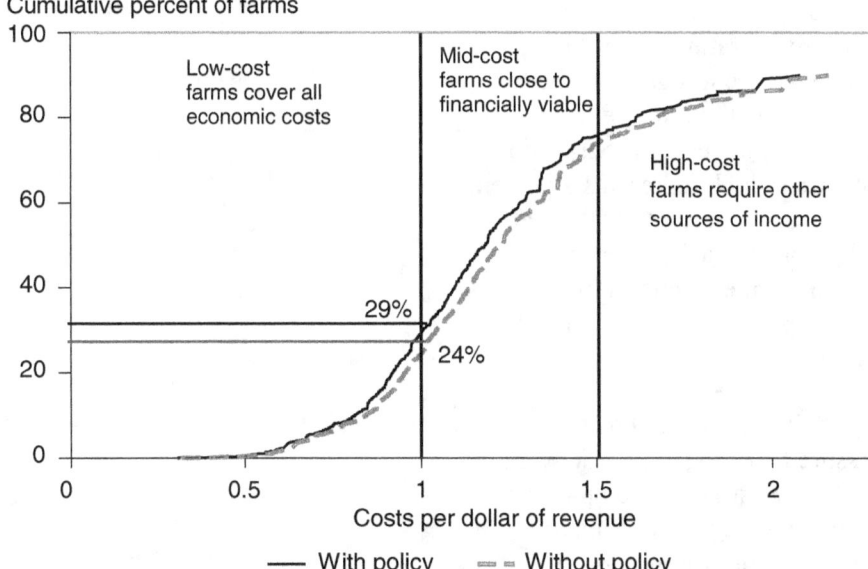

Cumulative percent of farms

- With policy   - - Without policy

National Dairy Programs' Effects on Food and Nutrition Programs

Effects of national dairy programs on food and nutrition (F&N) programs
(appendix D) arise through price effects on fluid milk and dairy products
either included directly in F&N programs or available with F&N program
assistance (GAO, 2001). The F&N programs involving large quantities of
fluid milk and other dairy products are affected most. Government costs for
dairy products provided by F&N programs are tied to individual dairy
product price indices and their contributions to the overall Consumer Price
Index.

Only the Special Supplemental Nutrition Program for Women, Infants, and
Children (WIC) is structured in such a way that higher dairy product prices
might reduce the number of participants. This is because WIC is a discretionary program funded by annual appropriations tied to F&N program
costs. The other F&N programs are entitlement programs where anyone
meeting the requirements can receive the benefits. Higher dairy prices
increase the cost of other government F&N programs and affect consumer
choices on how to spend their food dollars, which is particularly important
for the Food Stamp Program.

As shown in table 4.9, there are both positive and negative price effects
related to national dairy programs. At the wholesale level, national dairy
programs, as currently administered, tend to keep butter and cheese prices
lower while the price of nonfat dry milk and fluid milk is higher. Retail
prices mirror the effects seen at the wholesale level but are smaller in
percentage terms—fluid milk prices tend to be higher while dairy product
prices tend to be lower. The net effect of programs on costs (both to the
Government and to F&N program participants) depends on two things: the

shares of the products included in the programs and the consumers' buying behavior.

F&N programs where fluid milk is a major component will have higher dairy product costs, whether dairy programs are operating or not. It is critical to note that the full effects shown in table 4.9 are mitigated by how food cost indices are affected. For example, in situations where the Consumer Price Index for Urban workers (CPI-U) underlies program cost calculations, fluid milk carries a weight of .308 (which represents 2 percent of the food expenditure component of the CPI-U). Thus, a hypothetical 10-percent retail fluid milk price change would represent a 2-percent change in total food costs for the consumer. On the basis of the estimates in table 4.9, the range of effects from changes in fluid milk prices at retail on the CPI-U range from just under 1 to just over 2 percent.

In cases where expected higher costs due to dairy programs threatened to reduce participation, steps were taken to assure that program participants were not adversely affected. For example, Northeast Dairy Compact rules required reimbursements to the WIC program and the School Lunch Program for higher milk costs that resulted from Compact pricing. There is no corresponding requirement for Federal dairy programs.

National Dairy Program Effects on Rural Economies

U.S. dairy program impacts are felt not only on dairy farms but also in communities dependent on them for economic activity. National program effects on milk and dairy product prices and quantities derived from the aggregate national analyses described in a previous section are used to estimate impacts on dairy processing and other sectors of the economy as they are dispersed over regions of the country. The program effects on dairy industry indicators are used in an input-output framework to estimate the direct and indirect national impacts, and then distribute these impacts across

Table 4.9—Average wholesale and retail product price effects of dairy programs

	FAPRI	FAPSIM
	percent	
Wholesale		
Cheese	-2.8	-1.7
Butter	-16.5	-21.3
Nonfat dry milk	6.5	11.1
Retail		
Fluid	7.5	3.4
Cheese	-1.8	-0.4
Butter	-8.9	-9.4

Source: Brown (2003) and Price (2004).

State metro and nonmetro regions of the country. The effects of dairy programs on nonmetro areas are an indicator of their effects on rural economies.[5]

The estimated dairy program effects on milk and dairy product prices shown in table 4.1 generate an estimated $800 million in additional sales by dairy processors. Through inter-industry linkages, the added sales generate just over $2.2 billion in revenues nationwide, including the additional dairy product sales. Just over 25 percent of the additional sales revenue is by the farm sector in the form of dairy farm products and the additional feed. The added economic activity in the farm sector represents about 1.7 percent of dairy farm base revenues and about 1.4 percent of dairy processing base revenues (table 4.10).

There are employment effects associated with the additional economic activity generated by the dairy programs. The input-output model provides the estimated direct and indirect jobs effects by industry. The largest impacts are in the farm sector, which includes not only dairy farms but also farms that produce feed crops. Most of the jobs created as a result of dairy programs—over 65 percent—are in metro areas, but the impact in nonmetro areas is also significant. While nonmetro areas account for only 18 percent of all jobs in the U.S. economy, they account for 35 percent of the jobs created by U.S. dairy programs. The largest nonmetro impacts are in the North Central and the Plains regions, areas that are important locations for dairy farms, dairy processors, and feed crop production.

The estimated job effects of dairy programs on total employment are small on both national and regional levels, less than 0.1 percent in both cases. The effect on jobs in the dairy industry is higher percentage-wise, although still small. The added employment in dairy processing and manufacturing would be about 1 percent, while dairy farm employment increases by 1.5 percent.

[5]For definitions of "metro" and "nonmetro" see http://www.ers.usda.gov /Briefing/Rurality/ruralurbancon.

Table 4.10—National, regional, and county effects of dairy programs

	United States			Regional and county					
	Economic activity	Employment		Economic activity			Employment		
	Billion dollars	*1,000 jobs*		*Billion dollars*			*1,000 jobs*		
Total U.S.	2.20	13.1		Metro	Nonmetro	Total	Metro	Nonmetro	Total
Farm	0.56	5.2							
Dairy	0.37	3.4	Northeast	0.40	0.07	0.47	1.83	0.44	2.27
Livestock	0.00	0.0	North Central	0.42	0.26	0.67	2.15	1.87	4.02
Crops	0.19	1.7	Appalachia	0.12	0.07	0.19	0.59	0.38	0.97
Food processing	0.85	2.2	Southeast	0.19	0.07	0.26	1.01	0.42	1.43
Dairy processing	0.80	2.0	Plains	0.17	0.09	0.26	0.80	0.74	1.54
Other food processing	0.06	0.1	Mountain	0.09	0.05	0.14	0.48	0.39	0.87
Other manufacturing	0.32	1.2	Pacific	0.25	0.03	0.28	1.74	0.28	0.28
Trade and transportation	0.16	1.3							
Other services	0.33	3.3	Total U.S.	1.6	0.6	2.2	8.6	4.5	13.1

Source: USDA, ERS.
Note: Totals may not add due to rounding.

Most of the economic activity due to national dairy programs is distributed over the country in a pattern similar to the job effects (table 4.10). The largest nonmetro impacts are again in the North Central region. The estimated economic impacts are small on both the national and regional levels. However, even small effects for large regions may be important if they are centered in nonmetro areas where smaller communities depend on economic activity from dairy farms and dairy processing.

Summary

The quantitative analyses in this study examined national dairy program effects on market and farm-level indicators, the well-being of dairy farms, milk price volatility, food and nutrition (F&N) programs, and rural economic activity. Several empirical approaches were used because there is no comprehensive modeling framework available at this time that incorporates all of the relationships needed for the study.

The average effects of national dairy programs are modest. These results suggest that most market indicators are not sensitive to program intervention in the longer term. However, the results show that there are larger (on a percentage basis) shortrun effects in the early years as the industry adjusts to change. The results reflect the difficulty of modeling dramatic program changes when their effects are embedded in data and the assumptions and parameters underlying the analytical frameworks. It is possible that a market indicator, the all-milk price for example, might not differ from baseline values in the longer term as dairy programs are changed. Or, the divergence from baseline values might be significant. The key to making use of this type of analysis is examination of the revealed changes in market indicators from baseline conditions and the direction of those changes.

The analysis presented here is limited to effects on market variables—price, production, and consumption—and reveals little about program effects on the structure of the dairy sector. Dairy programs are estimated to raise the all-milk price by less than 2 percent on average over a 5- or 6-year period while cash receipts increase by about 3 to 4 percent. To the extent that higher prices keep some marginal milk producers in production, dairy programs may slow structural change at the farm level, which is also driven by technological advances and changing consumer demands. Technology, changing consumer demand, and changes in upstream and downstream sectors are more important determinants of the structural change seen in the dairy industry.

Price levels are not the only concern of milk producers and other dairy industry participants—volatility has become an issue as well. Price stability is a goal of some dairy programs. The dynamic simulation analysis provides some empirical evidence supporting that conjecture but more extensive work is needed. The MILC and dairy support programs do appear to reduce price volatility as measured by the standard deviation of selected milk and dairy product prices.

The results give us a first cut at some of the distributional effects of dairy programs. While the average effects of dairy programs may be small, the impacts are likely to vary according to the size and location of individual dairy farms. Results of farm-level analysis show that, on average, dairy farms are better off with dairy programs in effect. But that is not a universal result. A second analysis of farm viability suggests that a higher milk price would allow a larger share of farms to be profitable or viable in the short to medium term.

However, in the longer term, without dramatic changes in the cost structure of dairy farms, low-cost farmers will be more profitable with higher prices, but expanding production will drive milk prices lower. This result presents a quandary—it is not likely that all farms will be willing or able to be in the low-cost category. Given that situation, the solution to the long-term existence of medium- and high-cost farms may be direct payments to farmers meeting certain criteria rather than market intervention designed to affect prices. It is possible that budget exposure might also be reduced with a direct payment program. In that sense, current milk programs, except for MILC, may accelerate structural change.

Effects on food and nutrition (F&N) programs are mainly cost-related. In only one case, the Special Supplemental Nutrition Program for Women, Infants, and Children (WIC), is participation and cost linked in such a way as to possibly reduce participation as costs rise. The other F&N programs are entitlements and participation means essentially taking advantage of the benefits of the programs to obtain dairy products. In the case of food stamps, higher food costs affect consumer food demand which in and of itself does not necessarily reduce program participation. Higher food costs clearly could affect the share of food stamp dollars spent on dairy products.

In the context of regional economic effects, the modest national effects of dairy programs are distributed throughout the U.S. according to the importance of dairy farming and dairy-related sectors in local economies. Not surprisingly, the greatest effects are in areas where dairy farming and dairy production are still significant economic sectors. Also of interest are the measures of effects on metro areas where many milk processing or manufacturing operations are located. The fact that dairy programs affect change in all the components of the dairy industry (producers, processors, or manufacturers) contributes to this result.

Finally, forces other than dairy policy and programs—such as technology and changing consumer food preferences—are affecting the U.S. dairy industry, the effects of which are embedded in model structure, parameters, and data. These forces are likely to continue to move the dairy industry in the direction exhibited by long-term trends. The effects of some of these forces may be more important than the effects of national dairy programs on aggregate dairy market indicators.

An Alternative Milk Pricing Approach

Section 1508(A) of the 2002 Food Security and Rural Investment Act called for USDA to "conduct a study on the effects of—(1) terminating all Federal programs relating to price support and supply management; and (2) granting the consent of Congress to cooperative efforts by States to manage milk prices and supply." It is not clear what "cooperative efforts by States. . ." means specifically in the context of the request, but the *Northeast Interstate Dairy Compact (NEIDC,* or the Compact) that operated from July 1997 to September 2001 is a recent example of such an effort.[1] The NEIDC was a realization of the wide array of possibilities for defining compacts and their objectives.

[1]The NEIDC did not impose supply management but the issue was raised toward the end of its operation.

The answers to important economic questions regarding compacts rest on assessments of benefits and costs to stakeholders in the industry. Who gets the benefits and who bears the costs depends on the specific design of the compact arrangements. Legislation to reauthorize dairy compacts has been introduced periodically but not enacted. The congressional mandate in the 2002 Act offers an opportunity to review this program and to analyze the effects of its potential reintroduction under a particular set of assumptions.

The Northeast Interstate Dairy Compact

New York State legislators pressed for a dairy compact in the Northeast in the late 1980s. By 1993, the six New England States had passed the legislation required to form a Compact and the governors were in agreement. Congress consented to the Compact with the passage of the 1996 Federal Agriculture Improvement and Reform Act. Connecticut, Maine, Massachusetts, New Hampshire, Rhode Island, and Vermont were authorized to enter into the NEIDC as specified in section 1, Senate Joint Resolution 28 of the 104th Congress, subject to the Secretary of Agriculture finding compelling public interest in the Compact region.

The objectives of the NEIDC included: 1) increasing dairy farmer income to assure continued viability of dairy farming in the region; 2) assuring consumers in the region an adequate local supply of pure and wholesome milk; 3) encouraging the vitality of the region's rural economy; and 4) preserving open spaces. Farm milk price volatility and the effects of the Compact on wholesale and retail milk prices were also concerns. Fluid milk price regulation was the key—dairy farmers receiving a "fair and equitable" price for their milk would ensure an adequate local milk supply and continued vitality of the dairy industry. A commission was established to carry out the Compact's objectives.

The Compact commission's pricing authority was limited to Class I milk, the milk used in fluid beverage products. Table 5.1 shows the average[2] annual Compact price, the relevant Federal Milk Market Order (FMMO) price for Class I milk, and the Compact premium—the amount in excess of the FMMO price that processors were required to pay for Class I milk. Revenue generated by the Compact regulation was returned to eligible producers through a pooling mechanism.

[2]Calculations and Compact payments, when made, were on a monthly basis. See http:\\www.dairycompact.org for the monthly prices.

Table 5.1—Compact price, Federal order price, and Compact premium for Class 1 milk, annual average

Year	Compact price	Federal order price	Compact premium
	dollars per hundredweight		
1997[1]	16.94	14.91	2.03
1998	16.94	16.78	0.67
1999	16.94	16.90	1.20
2000	16.94	14.80	2.14
2001[2]	16.94	17.45	0.34

[1]July-December.
[2]January-September.
Source: Northeast Dairy Compact Commission.

Under the 1996 Act, the life of the Compact was linked to reform of FMMOs. Implementation of a reformed FMMO system as mandated by the 1996 Act would mark expiration of the Compact's authority. Congress broke this link by extending the Compact beyond the date the reformed FMMO system was put in place in January 2000 to September 2001.

What did the Northeast Interstate Dairy Compact do?[3]

The NEIDC was the subject of many research efforts. The results of several studies are summarized here and complete citations (or Internet links if available) are provided in the References for those wishing to access the original source material. The studies emphasized: farm-level effects, retail fluid milk price effects, and other dairy product price effects.

Farm-level effects. Production increases in response to higher product prices is an economic principle as applicable to dairy farms as to any other business. Alexander and Nicholson (2002) found that the mandated minimum NEIDC Class I price increased producer returns by an average $0.53 per hundredweight (cwt) over the applicable FMMO blend price over the life of the Compact. Nicholson et al. (2001) concluded that in its first year of operation, the Compact increased the region's milk production by about 1 percent. Since the Compact States accounted for only about 3 percent of total U.S. milk production, national impacts were negligible.

Expanding the area under Compact regulation would increase national effects. For example, expanding the NEIDC to the 11 States named in the 1996 Act as possible members would cover 11 percent of national production. Cox et al. (1999) analyzed the interregional impacts of an expanded NEIDC in the context of the dairy provisions as written in the 1996 Act. They found that adding $2.00 to the relevant FMMO Class I differential for the expanded NEIDC region would increase returns to the region's dairy farmers by $237 million but decrease returns in non-Compact regions by $146 million—an interregional producer and consumer wealth transfer of $383 million. Adding a southern compact would increase returns to the combined compact region's dairy farmers by $504 million but decrease

[3] Much of the material in this section is from Knutson et al. (2003).

returns in non-Compact regions by $340 million—an interregional producer and consumer wealth transfer of $844 million.[4]

Retail fluid milk price effects. Food prices tend to be "sticky" downward, meaning they readily rise when farm prices rise but are slow to decline when farm prices drop. Outlaw et al. (1994) and Hall et al. (1993) reported finding little relationship between prices producers receive for their products and retail prices. Brand (1963) and Padberg et al. (1993) found that pricing decisions made by food processors, supermarket operators, and other food retailers involve complex issues that have little direct relationship to farm prices. Because of retail price stickiness, analyzing the effects of compacts, particularly on consumers, may not be straightforward.

If higher Class I milk prices to fluid milk processors are indeed passed on to retailers, it is reasonable to expect higher consumer prices for fluid milk. Studies verify that this happened in the NEIDC on at least a penny-for-penny basis. Lass et al. (2001) found that average retail price increases in Boston, MA and Hartford, CT were about equal to increases in processors' milk input costs. However, Cotterill and Franklin (2001) found supermarket prices were higher than could be explained by increases in Class I milk prices due to the Compact. Neither study analyzed milk prices or price spreads over the entire Compact period.

There were occasions during the life of the Compact when the relevant FMMO Class I minimum price rose above or fell below the minimum Compact Class I price. Retail milk prices did not decrease as rapidly when the prices fell—a consequence of stickiness as noted above. In any event, the increase in the price of milk was estimated by Cox to result in less than a 1-percent reduction in the region's demand for fluid milk.

Retail prices reported by FMMO Administrators and processor/retailer price spreads for whole and 2-percent milk for two Compact markets (Hartford, CT and Boston, MA) and four non-Compact markets (Atlanta, GA, Chicago, IL, Dallas, TX, and Seattle, WA) were analyzed for the period between January 1994 and October 2002.[5] When adjusted for labor and fuel costs and seasonality, the processor/retailer price spreads were no higher for either whole milk or 2-percent milk in the Compact markets than in the non-Compact markets. Of the six markets studied, price spreads were lowest in Boston (by $0.10 per gallon) and Hartford (by $0.09 per gallon) during the Compact period. Following the Compact period, the processor/retailer price spread widened by $0.068 per gallon on whole milk and $0.074 per gallon on 2-percent milk as the cooperative price fell by $0.12 per gallon in the Compact markets. However, it is important to note that the spread increased even more in the non-Compact markets—by $0.093 per gallon on whole milk and $0.108 per gallon on 2-percent milk. These results suggest that retail prices indeed were sticky in the Compact markets, but they were even stickier in the non-Compact markets (Knutson et al., 2003).

[4]The same type of interregional wealth transfers occurs when FMMO Class I price differentials are increased. This occurs because of regional differences in fluid utilization among markets. While liberal pooling provisions reduce the distortions in producer revenues, they do not eliminate the distortions in product prices.

[5]Retail prices were those reported by the USDA's Agricultural Marketing Service (AMS) which, because of limited sampling, may not reflect an average city or municipal area price. For the Compact markets, the retail price worksheets, provided by AMS, were used to calculate the Compact price differential, which was added to the AMS's cooperative Class I quoted price. All city prices were adjusted to the designated 3.25-percent or 2-percent butterfat and converted to a price per gallon. The price spread was the gallon retail price minus the milk cost.

Other dairy product price effects. The combination of increased milk supply and reduced demand for Class I milk, both due to a higher Compact price, affects not only fluid milk markets but other dairy product markets as well. Increased production results in a spillover into manufacturing use, which would be expected to reduce dairy product prices. Cox et al. (1999) found that under alternative scenarios related to an expanded NEIDC, a Southern Compact, and a combined NEIDC/Southern Compact, average manufactured dairy product prices generally fell, particularly for American cheese ($0.07 to $0.174 per pound) and nonfat dry milk ($0.115 to $0.384 per pound). Butter prices actually increased somewhat.

The previous analyses we have reviewed and summarized all concluded that certain producers—those supplying milk to the Compact area—received extra income through Compact premium payments. However, these benefits generated costs for other segments of the dairy industry both inside and outside the Compact. Higher fluid milk prices inside the Compact raised costs to consumers in the Compact area and led to efforts by the Compact Commission to offset them, at least for some consumers (those in the WIC program for example). Reduced fluid milk consumption due to the higher prices made more milk available for manufacturing so that dairy product prices, on the whole, declined somewhat. If production in the Compact region expanded at a rate greater than the national average and price support purchases were occurring, the Compact producers had to cover that added CCC product purchase cost. Lower product prices also affected producers outside the Compact(s) by lowering the value of milk in manufacturing uses. Expanding the area under compact programs implied greater adjustments by non-Compact producers

Compacts in Lieu of Federal Dairy Programs

Termination of the NEIDC in 2001 did not quell interest in dairy compacts. In January 2003, legislation was introduced in the House of Representatives calling for restoring the consent of Congress to the Compact and granting consent to a Southern Dairy Compact, a Pacific Northwest Dairy Compact, and an Intermountain Dairy Compact.[6] The analysis in this report is based on a scenario similar to the January 2003 proposal. For our analysis, three Compacts are defined: the Northeast, the Southern, and the Western. There are non-Compact areas in the scenario we have chosen to consider. More will be said about these areas in a following section.

The analytical framework

The interregional impacts of alternative U.S. dairy policies and programs have been examined using the University of Wisconsin-Madison Dairy Sector Interregional Competition Model (UW-IRCM). The model is designed to represent regional supply and demand conditions and dairy policies in the United States at particular points in time. It relies on the FMMOs and California as the basis for spatial definitions and makes extensive use of milk component balancing and pricing.[7]

Two "policy bases," 2000 BASE and 2001 BASE, were derived to characterize the U.S. dairy industry under recent low-price (2000) and high-price (2001) supply and demand situations. The base-year models have been

[6]The legislation, H.R. 324, was introduced January 8, 2003, by Representative Vitter of Louisiana and was referred to the Committee on the Judiciary.

[7]Additional details about the UW-IRCM can be found in Cox and Chavas (2001) and Chavas et al. (1998).

adjusted to reflect current (2002) program features so that the empirical results represent changes from a base that includes current programs. The simulations of the base years include the following current policy or program features: FMMO pricing as implemented in 2000 for 11 FMMOs; support price at $9.90 per cwt with the butter-powder tilt as in 2002; California pricing rules and MILC payments as defined under the program. The MILC payments were retained given the interpretation that the only Federal program eliminated was milk price support. More will be said about the implications of this assumption in the sections reporting empirical results. Trade-related policies and programs are unchanged from those in place in 2002. The base-year simulations are calibrated to U.S. and California production and prices in the base years as well as commodity reference prices, an example being the Chicago Mercantile Exchange price for cheese (Cox and Dabidia, 2003).

Defining compacts for analysis

Several States have either expressed strong interest in or have passed legislation for participating in potential interregional dairy compact programs. The UW-IRCM model cannot precisely incorporate some individual States' potential participation in an interstate dairy compact. However, by allocating these States to the existing FMMO regions defined in the UW-IRCM framework, Compacts may be defined.

The three Compact regions formed for our analysis are the Northeast, the Southern, and the Western. The Northeast includes the six New England States plus New York and Pennsylvania. The Southern is comprised of North Carolina, South Carolina, Georgia, Alabama, Mississippi, Louisiana, Arkansas, Tennessee, Missouri, Kentucky, Oklahoma, Kansas, Nebraska, South Dakota, Iowa, Illinois, and Colorado. It is by far the largest Compact, at least in terms of geographic area. Finally, the Western Compact includes Idaho, Utah, Nevada, Washington, Oregon, and California. The Upper Midwest, Mideast, Southwest, Arizona and Florida FMMO regions do not directly participate in the defined compacts.

There are other key issues involved with modeling compacts, including the target Class I price, pooling provisions, and how milk from outside compact areas is addressed. The Compact Class I target price is assumed to be $16.94 per cwt in all three compact areas. If the relevant FMMO Class I price is below the Compact Class I target price, processors must pay a compact premium into the compact region's producer settlement pool which in turn will be distributed back to producers.

As for milk entering from outside compacts and compact pooling provisions, the UW-IRCM framework includes neither individual farms nor plants, so the pooling provisions are difficult to model well. As the NEIDC illustrated, milk produced outside the Compact area still entered that area and was subject to Compact pricing rules. The analysis here is based on assumed full compact border protection which simplifies the analysis and provides "upper-bound" simulation results. There are also some restrictions on movements of milk among areas within compact areas that limit extreme results that run counter to well-established relationships.

Simulation results

The alternative dairy policy scenario posits elimination of the Federal dairy price support program and authorization for three compacts to carry out milk pricing functions (Cox and Dabidia, 2003). The empirical results discussed here are presented in tables 5.2 through 5.4. The model solutions represent intermediate run (3-5 years) adjustments to the base scenarios induced by policy changes and/or supply- or demand-generated shocks The implications for the farm level, the wholesale/processing and manufacturing level, wholesale and classified prices, government costs, and welfare measures are described. **For analyses such as the one presented here it is critical to remember that changes from the base year variable levels are important, not the actual levels of the variables that appear.**

Farm-level effects

The U.S. average farm milk price (the average over all classes and including MILC payments) declines from the 2000 base by almost 3 percent with the elimination of Federal price support and establishment of three compact areas (table 5.2). The results are presented in terms of the FMMO regions that still underlie the definitions of the Compact regions in the model plus California. The nationwide manufacturing milk price declines and fluid milk price declines in non-Compact regions outweigh the MILC payment increases. Aggregate production rises by about 0.4 percent (compact region increases exceed non-Compact region decreases), while revenues (market returns plus MILC payments) fall by 2.5 percent.

Relatively wide variations in percentage measures of change are observed across the spatial regions in the model. California shows the largest price decrease while the largest increase is in the Southeast. Recall that California's State pricing regulations are unchanged. The implementation of a Western Compact does not preclude operation of the State's own classified pricing plan, just as no elimination of Federal milk marketing orders is proposed. The Compact-pricing rule refers to Class I utilization for a much wider area. In addition, since such a large percentage of California production goes into manufactured products, the elimination of a program that directly affects those products would be expected to have an impact. Production, on a percentage basis, declines the most in Arizona and increases the most in the Southeast. Regional revenue changes mirror the price changes.

Compared with the 2001 base, reflecting a high-price situation, the average U.S. price rises less than 1 percent, as do production and revenue. Price declines in the non-Compact areas are smaller relative to the 2001 base situation (table 5.2) and regional price changes are smaller in percentage terms. The price still declines most in California, but by only 2.5 percent, and increases 10.4 percent in the Southeast. Changes in production and revenues are also less than in the 2000 base case—only in the Southeast is any production change greater than 1 percent in either direction. Revenue falls most in Arizona (2.9 percent) and the increase is greatest in the Southeast (15 percent).

The pattern of gains and losses among the regions exhibits one clear feature—the Southeast subarea of the larger Southeastern Compact benefits

Table 5.2—Farm level changes relative to bases under selected compact scenario

	Base			Scenario[1]		
	All-milk price +MILC	Production	Total revenues	All-milk price +MILC	Production	Total revenues
	$ per cwt	Million pounds	Million $	Percent change from base		
2000 (low-price year)						
Northeast	13.92	29,460	4,101	2.5	0.7	3.2
Appalachia	14.97	6,492	972	13.9	9.0	24.2
Florida **	15.39	2,852	439	-10.5	-4.3	-14.4
Southeast	13.40	5,429	733	23.7	9.6	35.5
Mideast **	13.34	12,762	1,702	-7.3	-2.4	-9.5
Upper Midwest **	12.46	33,665	4,195	-7.1	-2.3	-9.2
Central	12.73	14,089	1,794	2.6	1.1	3.7
Southwest **	12.75	10,853	1,384	-8.6	-3.3	-11.6
Western	11.04	9,792	1,081	-3.7	-1.6	-5.3
Northwest	12.50	7,151	894	1.8	0.8	2.6
California	11.12	32,146	3,575	-13.0	3.3	-10.2
Arizona **	11.59	2,943	341	-12.8	-4.9	-17.0
Aggregate U.S.	12.65	167,634	21,210	-2.9	0.4	-2.5
FMMO all-market uniform price	13.02			-0.7		
2001 (high-price year)						
Northeast	15.42	28,146	4,340	1.9	0.6	2.6
Appalachia	16.22	6,237	1,012	-0.3	-0.2	-0.5
Florida **	17.01	2,365	402	-1.4	-0.5	-1.7
Southeast	15.12	5,104	772	10.4	4.1	15.0
Mideast **	14.94	12,727	1,901	-1.7	-0.6	-2.3
Upper Midwest **	14.17	30,808	4,365	-0.4	-0.1	-0.6
Central	14.50	13,142	1,906	0.7	0.3	0.9
Southwest **	14.19	10,287	1,460	-0.2	-0.1	-0.3
Western	12.63	9,893	1,249	-0.1	0.0	-0.1
Northwest	14.21	6,972	991	1.9	0.8	2.6
California	13.01	32,619	4,244	-2.5	0.1	-2.4
Arizona **	13.54	2,794	378	-2.1	-0.8	-2.9
Aggregate U.S.	14.29	161,094	23,020	0.1	0.2	0.3
FMMO all-market uniform price	14.61			0.7		

[1]The scenario posits establishment of three Compact areas as defined in the text and elimination of the Federal price support program. MILC is assumed to be in effect.
** denotes areas that are NOT under Compact pricing rules.
Source: Cox and Dabidia (2003).

regardless of the initial price situation. The results for the other subareas of the Southeastern Compact are mixed—all the subareas benefit in the low-price case but in the high-price case the Appalachian subarea shows a decrease in price. Regions without compacts (Florida, the Mideast, the Upper Midwest, the Southwest, and Arizona) lose when compacts are initiated and Federal dairy price support is eliminated. Increased milk production in response to higher milk prices and reduced fluid milk demand in compact areas have spillover effects in the manufacturing milk market which are no longer mitigated by price support activities. These impacts are greater in a low-price supply and demand context, e.g. 2000, than a high-price context, e.g. 2001. Some of these 2000 (versus 2001) regional revenue losses are substantial: the Mideast (-9.5 percent vs. -2.3 percent); the Upper Midwest (-9.2 percent vs. -0.6 percent); and California (-10.2 percent vs. -2.4 percent).

Wholesale/processing and manufacturing level effects

Elimination of the dairy price support program results in decreased whole-sale prices for all products except fluid milk and butter compared with the base scenarios (table 5.3). All the prices are national averages, i.e. averaged over all the regional results. Average fluid milk prices increase 11.9 percent for the 2000 base situation and butter is up 3.2 percent. The higher fluid prices in the compacts generate an average 1.6-percent decline in fluid milk production (which generally is assumed equal to consumption). As more milk becomes available for manufactured products, production increases, but not in all cases. The price increases for fluid milk and butter are 7.6 and 2 percent, respectively, in the 2001 base situation, with fluid consumption down 1 percent.

The importance of the dairy price support program in a low-price year is evident in the comparison of the reduction in American cheese prices (-12.9 percent in 2000 vs. -3.1 percent in 2001), and nonfat dry milk prices (-28.6 percent vs. -5.3 percent). American cheese production falls 4.3 percent in the 2000 case and increases slightly in the 2001 case. Aggregate U.S. wholesale dairy product revenues decrease 2.4 percent under 2000 market conditions while increasing 0.6 percent under 2001 conditions. Fluid milk processors' revenues increase in both cases, by 10 percent for 2000 and by 6.5 percent for 2001.

Classified prices

Given the drops in the wholesale prices of American cheese and nonfat dry milk in the two scenarios, FMMO Class III and California Class 4b prices fall about 17 and 13.4 percent, respectively, from the 2000 base, and 4.1 and 3.2 percent, respectively, from the 2001 base (table 5.4). FMMO Class IV and California Class 4a prices fall by 15 and 16 percent, respectively, (2000) and 2.7 and 2.7 percent (2001). These lower classified prices generate considerably less regional price differences that are offset by larger compact premiums and larger MILC payments. Assessing these offsetting impacts analytically is very difficult.

Government costs and economic surplus measures

Because the scenario posits elimination of the Federal dairy price support program, CCC costs drop sharply (-62.3 percent) in 2000, and are elimi-nated in 2001 (table 5.4). However, removing CCC purchase program costs tends to raise other costs, including MILC program costs. Lower Class III and Class IV (manufacturing milk) prices in FMMOs—the Class I price movers—reduce relevant Class I reference prices in compacts, thereby increasing both the compact premium and the MILC payment rate. MILC

Table 5.3—Wholesale level changes relative to bases under selected compact scenario

	Base			Scenario[1]		
	Production	Price	Revenues	Production	Price	Revenues
	Million pounds	*Dollars per cwt*	*Million dollars*	*Percent change from base*		
2000 (low-price year)						
Fluid	55,415	12.64	6,936	-1.6	11.9	10.0
Soft products	7,712	26.76	2,044	2.9	-6.9	-4.3
American cheese	3,837	112.00	3,965	-4.3	-12.9	-11.2
Italian cheese	2,664	78.59	2,079	4.1	-16.9	-13.5
Other cheese	1,312	93.87	1,415	8.4	-16.1	-9.9
Butter	1,214	131.48	1,542	-0.9	3.2	2.1
Frozen	11,976	20.80	2,465	2.3	-7.8	-7.1
Other manufactured	4,293	26.70	1,152	0.7	-3.1	-2.4
NFDM	1,365	81.53	633	4.1	-28.6	-21.8
Aggregate U.S.			22,231			-2.4
2001 (high-price year)						
Fluid	54,569	13.03	7,105	-1.0	7.6	6.5
Soft products	6,924	30.21	2,090	0.4	-0.9	-0.6
American cheese	3,540	133.59	4,872	0.5	-3.1	-2.7
Italian cheese	2,704	110.23	2,921	0.8	-3.3	-2.5
Other cheese	1,338	126.38	2,045	1.7	-2.8	-1.4
Butter	809	162.46	2,029	0.1	2.0	1.6
Frozen	12,256	24.47	2,983	0.1	-1.3	-1.2
Other manufactured	3,892	41.22	1,318	0.8	-4.0	-3.1
NFDM	978	83.96	817	1.8	-5.3	-3.4
Aggregate U.S.			26,179			0.6

[1]The scenario posits establishment of three Compact areas as defined in the text and elimination of the Federal price support program. MILC is assumed to be in effect.
Source: Cox and Dabidia (2003).

program costs rise by 57.5 percent from the 2000 base, and almost 24 percent from the 2001 base. Due to the increased compact premiums and increased MILC payments, producer surplus increases slightly (0.6 percent for 2000, 0.7 percent for 2001). Hence, while producer prices decline, other programs operating under the scenario—compacts and MILC—can, at least partially, offset this negative impact.

Consumer welfare is negatively affected by higher fluid milk prices in compact areas but lower classified and commodity prices mitigate the effects. The net impact of these offsetting effects is a consumer surplus gain (1.5 percent) in the 2000 case, but a loss (0.2 percent) in the 2001 case. Given the change in government costs due to the MILC program, aggregate U.S. welfare increases 0.8 percent under 2000 conditions but falls by 0.1 percent in the 2001 case.

Table 5.4—Changes in selected variables under selected compact scenario[1]

Classified pricing

	Base values ($ per cwt)	Change from base (Percent)
2000 (low-price year)		
Class I	13.38	-12.3
Class II	11.49	-14.4
Class III	9.29	-17.1
Class IV	10.79	-15.3
CA Class I	12.29	-13.5
CA Class 2	11.02	-15.0
CA Class 4	10.89	-15.2
CA Class 4a	10.53	-15.8
CA Class 4b	9.47	-13.4
2001 (high-price year)		
Class I	14.87	-2.2
Class II	12.98	-2.5
Class III	11.93	-4.1
Class IV	12.28	-2.7
CA Class I	14.65	-2.3
CA Class 2	11.96	-2.8
CA Class 4	13.01	-2.5
CA Class 4a	12.21	-2.7
CA Class 4b	11.75	-3.2

Commodity reference prices

	Base values ($ per cwt)	Change from base (Percent)
2000		
NASS american cheese	111.33	-11.5
CME american cheese	112.83	-11.5
NASS butter	132.25	6.0
CME butter	136.42	6.0
NASS nonfat dry milk	80.10	-29.2
CME nonfat dry milk	81.57	-29.2
NASS whey	0.15	-33.3
2001		
NASS american cheese	133.90	-2.9
CME american cheese	135.05	-2.9
NASS butter	164.96	1.4
CME butter	168.26	1.4
NASS nonfat dry milk	81.28	-6.1
CME nonfat dry milk	84.52	-6.1
NASS whey	0.22	-4.5

Surplus-welfare measures

	Base values (Million $)	Change from base (Percent)
2000		
Producer surplus	17,216	0.6
Consumer surplus	56,466	1.5
CCC costs	591	-62.3
Other govt costs	1,290	57.5
Total welfare	71,080	0.8
2001		
Producer surplus	18,695	0.7
Consumer surplus	67,908	-0.2
CCC costs	1	-100.0
Other govt costs	595	23.9
Total welfare	86,007	-0.1

[1]The scenario posits establishment of three Compact areas as defined in the text and elimination of the Federal price support program. MILC is assumed to be in effect.
Source: Cox and Dabidia (2003).

Summary

The analysis suggests that compacts can generate substantive gains to their regions and that these gains will be larger in years with lower prices. Compacts increase Class I price differences among regions. To the extent that compacts increase regional milk prices, regional milk production increases while the higher Class I prices lead to reduced fluid milk consumption. This generates more milk that must find an outlet in the manufacturing product sector, hence reducing manufactured dairy product prices. Regions with substantial manufacturing use generally suffer losses due to this type of policy. Consumers of fluid milk in compact areas lose due to higher Class I prices in the compact regions, while consumers of manufactured dairy products tend to gain due to the spillovers of extra milk on manufacturing markets, which lowers manufactured dairy product prices. In aggregate, however, consumers lose due to higher expenditure on Class I milk dominating reduced manufactured expenditures.

Direct payment programs like the 2002 MILC program can partially offset losses (or enhance the gains) due to compacts, but there is a cost. That cost is borne by taxpayers in the form of the direct government payments. Whenever the Class I price mover is reduced relative to the MILC target price, then the MILC payments will be increased. This is evident in the scenario presented here—eliminating the dairy price support program results in lower prices for all classes of milk (by lowering both the Class III and Class IV prices). However, with compacts in place, lowering the Class I price mover will increase the compact premium and offset the lower overall reduction in class prices in those regions with compacts. Under the constraints we have placed on the empirical model here, it appears elimination of the Federal price support program, which underpins all producer prices, results in price effects that Compact payments and MILC payments do not offset. If the compacts were to try to address these negative price effects, they would have the same options available to the Federal Government—they could operate a purchase program (unlikely) or attempt to manage supply. Whether supply management could be implemented at some subnational level is open to question.

The scenario employed in this analysis is similar to a proposal made in January 2003 to reauthorize and expand compacts. The scenario envisioned the existence of non-Compact areas and employed some rather restrictive assumptions to derive empirical estimates of the effects on dairy industry market indicators (e.g., prices and production). The net impacts of gains and losses will vary by region, depending on several factors. Those factors include whether the region has a compact; the magnitude of Class I sales and/or utilization, the shares of milk going into manufactured products (especially cheese and nonfat dry milk), the shares of milk production eligible for MILC payments, and interregional competitiveness.

There are obvious alternative specifications of this scenario. It could be hypothesized that compact pricing across the areas defined would not be the same. There could also be more or fewer compacts defined. The retention of the MILC payment program for all producers could be modified so that only non-Compact producers, in cases where there are such areas, would receive them. Or, MILC payments could be eliminated. Each individual scenario that might be considered has its own unique features to be incorporated in an empirical analysis.

Even if compacts covered the entire country, there would still be gains and losses. Compacts could not readily restrict commerce so that the prices received by producers in any one area could be the result of marketing activities in another. Compacts do not inherently alter sales patterns or utilization rates. And, competitiveness among producers, regardless of location, will still be linked to local conditions that affect production costs. The contrasts between the results for a low-price year (2000) and for a high-price year (2001) are as expected—contemplated or hypothesized dairy policy changes have smaller effects in periods of strong prices.

Implications for State Pricing and State-Mandated Over-Order Premiums

State pricing and over-order premium programs bear many similarities to interstate compacts. Like State pricing programs, which operate in conjunction with, or in lieu of, Federal milk marketing orders, the Compact analysis assumed that Federal marketing orders remained in effect. Most State pricing programs, like the hypothetical compacts analyzed in this chapter, establish Class I milk prices.

The analysis of interstate compacts can provide some insights into the effects of some State pricing and State-mandated over-order premium programs. State pricing programs that establish Class I prices above the prevailing Federal market order price in surrounding States raise the price of fluid milk to consumers in the State and reduce fluid consumption. Higher fluid milk prices may induce an increase in milk production, which finds an outlet in manufacturing use. If the spillover to the manufacturing market is large, manufacturing milk prices could fall, as they do in the hypothetical compact example. In this instance, producers in States without pricing programs would be adversely affected.

However, there are several important differences between compacts and State programs. While the compact analysis assumed that all compacts used the same price for Class I milk, existing State pricing programs may have different prices. The compacts regulate only Class I milk, while some States (like California) regulate other milk classes. And while the analysis assumed that compacts augment the Class I price, some State pricing programs—notably California—may result in Class I prices below those of the surrounding Federal marketing order market areas.

Conclusions

Dairy Policy Has a Modest Impact

An examination of dairy program impacts suggests that Federal dairy programs raise the all-milk price by only about 1 percent, and raise total producer revenues (returns plus Government payments) by 3 percent, on average, over 5 years. While producers are, as a whole, better off with dairy programs, these programs do raise consumer costs, albeit modestly, and increase Government expenditures.

The analysis shows that current programs both increase and decrease the all-milk price. The Milk Income Loss Contract (MILC) program, by increasing producer returns through production-linked payments, expands production, and reduces the milk price. Without the MILC program, the remaining dairy programs raise the all-milk price by a greater amount—4 percent as opposed to about 1 percent—on average over 5 years.

Federal dairy programs, by increasing farm-level returns, may enable high-cost farms to remain in business longer. But higher prices can only improve the viability of high-cost farms in the short to medium term. In the longer run, high-cost farms will have difficulty competing with low-cost dairy producers. Higher prices improve the profitability of low-cost dairy producers, which may enable them to expand production and gain market share.

The stability of prices and returns is especially important to dairy farms since, on average, they tend to be less diversified and more dependent on income from the farm business than other farms. Intervention's impact on farms varies regionally. An analysis of dairy program effects on the financial conditions of representative farms around the United States reveals that the current policy structure may lower the returns of some Western dairies.

Dairy programs raise the retail price of fluid milk, which affects both consumer expenditures on food and the cost of operating food and nutrition programs. In the case of the Special Supplemental Nutrition Program for Women, Infants, and Children (WIC), it is possible that higher fluid milk prices could affect participation. Because WIC is a discretionary grant program funded by annual appropriations, the number of participants depends on the appropriation and the cost of operating the program. Other food and nutrition programs are entitlement programs, and their costs are indexed to price indices that increase Government outlays when dairy programs raise product prices. Higher dairy prices are therefore unlikely to affect participation, but could affect how food stamp recipients choose to spend their food dollars.

National dairy programs have almost no impact on aggregate economic activity. Both nationally and at a broad regional level the industry's impact on employment is less than one-tenth of 1 percent of total employment. In areas that are highly dependent on milk production, impacts are likely to be greater. Because farm input (like machinery and fertilizer) production is located in metropolitan areas—as is much of the upstream processing and distribution activity—dairy programs very likely have greater impacts on metropolitan than on nonmetropolitan employment.

State Management of Milk Supplies and Prices Raises Difficult Issues

Unlike most other agricultural commodity markets, milk markets have a long history of State intervention. However, as milk markets have become increasingly integrated across State boundaries, the potential for effective State-level intervention in dairy markets has diminished. Today, of the major milk-producing States, only California and Pennsylvania set minimum prices for milk to any great extent.

The analysis of a State-level mechanism for managing milk prices extends the model of the Northeast Interstate Dairy Compact (NEIDC) by hypothesizing the formation of three interstate compacts. The study assumes that these compacts are implemented while eliminating the Federal milk price support program (there is no Federal supply management of milk) but all other programs—primarily MILC and Federal milk marketing orders—are assumed to remain in place.

In general, compacts establish a minimum price that processors are required to pay for Class I milk, the milk used in fluid beverage products. When this compact price is greater than the Federal Milk Marketing Order price, the difference (or some share of it) is returned to producers selling milk in the compact region. Higher returns to these producers lead to increased milk production and lower fluid milk consumption as consumers react to the higher retail prices. The resulting excess supply of milk above fluid requirements within the compact region spills over to the manufacturing milk market. As a result, manufacturing milk prices decline, as does the price of fluid milk in areas outside the compacts. These effects are greatest during low-price years.

As long as fluid utilization is high enough, returns to dairy farmers supplying the compact region increase as the higher fluid milk price more than offsets any decline in the price of manufacturing milk. However, lower manufacturing milk prices are felt nationally and the returns to dairy farmers outside the compact region decline. Farmers in regions with higher levels of manufacturing use for their milk suffer the greatest losses from this type of program because they do not receive a MILC payment that dampens the loss of revenues from fluid milk.

Consumers both outside and within the compact region benefit from lower prices for manufactured dairy products. However, consumers within compact regions spend more on fluid milk, while consumers outside the compact region would spend less on fluid milk.

Regional compacts may substitute for price support within these regions, as long as a large proportion of production is sold into the higher-priced fluid milk market, but are unlikely to substitute for price support on a national level. Extending compacts across the entire country would increase the impact on national milk production. Without some form of supply control, higher fluid prices applied to all producers would induce increased milk production that would spill over to the manufacturing milk market, driving down the price of milk for manufacturing use even further. The average producer price across all uses would decline further, rendering price management efforts ineffective.

This analysis raises questions regarding other means of State support. Were States to pursue a support program similar to the Federal milk price support program, States would need to address program funding, establish price support levels, and, if product purchase programs were implemented, dispose of surplus stocks. If supply control programs were adopted, additional considerations include establishing and enforcing quota levels and penalties or incentives for compliance. Such systems raise questions regarding cross-border issues—how to deal with milk flowing to areas with different price support or quota levels. While State or regional management of milk prices has received considerable attention as a possible alternative to current policy, this analysis suggests that it likely raises even more difficult issues than current policy.

References

Alexander, Craig, and Charles Nicholson, "Interstate Dairy Compacts," Extension Education Committee, National Institute for Livestock and Dairy Policy and Cornell Program on Dairy Markets and Policy, Cornell University, Ithaca, NY, 2002.

Alexander, Craig, John Siebert, David Anderson, and Ron Knutson. "State Milk Marketing Order Regulation and Interstate Dairy Compacts." Dairy Markets and Policy: Issues and Options, Cornell University Program on Dairy Markets and Policy, No. O-11, Ithaca, NY, October 1998.

Anderson, David P., Joe L. Outlaw, and Robert B. Schwart. "Structural Change in the Dairy Industry." Paper presented to Looking Ahead...or Looking Behind? 10th Annual Workshop for Dairy Economists and Policy Analysts. Memphis, TN, April 23-24, 2003, http://www.dairy.cornell.edu/CPDMP/Pages/Workshops/Memphis03/Anderson.pdf.

Bailey, Kenneth W. *Impact of MPC Imports on 2002 U.S. Cheese Production.* Staff Paper 362. Department of Agricultural Economics and Rural Sociology, The Pennsylvania State University, University Park, PA, March 2003.

_____. "Impact of the Northeast Dairy Compact on Consumer Prices for Fluid Milk." *Review of Agricultural Economics.* Volume 25, Number 1, 2003, pp. 108-122.

_____. *Implications of Dairy Imports: The Case of Milk Protein Concentrates.* Staff Paper 353. Department of Agricultural Economics and Rural Sociology, The Pennsylvania State University, University Park, PA, June 2002.

_____. *Imports of Milk Protein Concentrates: Assessing the Consequences.* Staff Paper 343. Department of Agricultural Economics and Rural Sociology, The Pennsylvania State University, University Park, PA, November 2001.

Balagtas, Joseph V., Bradley J. Rickard, and Daniel A. Sumner. "Effects of Proposed Trade Barriers for Milk Protein Concentrate and Casein Imports on the U.S. Dairy Industry." Paper presented at American Agricultural Economics Association annual meeting, Long Beach, CA. July 28-31, 2002.

Balagtas, Joseph V., and Daniel A. Sumner. "Forces Shaping the U.S. Dairy Industry," University of California, Davis, unpublished manuscript, April 2003.

_____. "The Effect of the Northeast Dairy Compact on Producers and Consumers, with Implications of Compact Contagion." *Review of Agricultural Economics.* Volume 25, Number 1, 2003, pp. 123-144.

Blayney, Don P. *The Changing Landscape of U.S. Milk Production*. U.S. Department of Agriculture, Economic Research Service. Statistical Bulletin No. 978, June 2002 (a).

_____. "Structural Changes in Fluid Milk Processing Continue." *Livestock, Dairy and Poultry Outlook*. U.S. Department of Agriculture, Economic Research Service, LDP-M-101. November 2002 (b).

Blayney, Don P., and Alden C. Manchester. "Large Companies Active in Changing Dairy Industry." *FoodReview*, Volume 23, Issue 2. U.S. Department of Agriculture, Economic Research Service, May-August 2000.

Blayney, Don P., and James Miller. "Concentration and Structural Change in Dairy Processing and Manufacturing." Paper presented to Looking Ahead...or Looking Behind? 10th Annual Workshop for Dairy Economists and Policy Analysts. Memphis, TN, April 23-24, 2003, http://www.dairy.cornell.edu/CPDMP/Pages/Workshops/Memphis03/Blayney.pdf.

Blayney, Don P., James J. Miller, and Richard P. Stillman. *Dairy: Background for 1995 Farm Legislation*. U. S. Department of Agriculture, Economic Research Service, Agricultural Economic Report No. 705, April 1995.

Boynton, Robert D. "Milk Marketing in California." Dairy Institute of California, Sacramento, CA, February 1992.

Brand, E.A. *Modern Supermarket Operation*. Fairchild Publications, New York, NY, 1963.

Brown, S. "The Effect on the United States Dairy Industry of Removing Current Federal Regulations." Food and Agricultural Policy Research Institute, University of Missouri, Columbia, MO, FAPRI-UMC report #03-03, April 2003.

Butler, L.J. "How did California become king of milk mountain?" *Hoard's Dairyman*, March 10, 2002.

_____. *Maintaining the Competitive Edge*. University of California—Agricultural Issues Center. 1992.

_____. "The California Make Allowance," Testimony submitted to the House Agriculture subcommittee on Livestock, Dairy and Poultry, Washington, DC, April 30, 1990.

California Department of Food and Agriculture. *California Dairy Industry Statistics*, 1950-1998.

_____. *California Dairy Information Bulletin*, December issues, 1950-1998.

California Department of Food and Agriculture, Dairy Marketing Branch. "California Milk Pricing Formulas," http://www.cdfa.ca.gov/dairy/pdf/SP108_Milk_PricFormulas_2003.pdf.

Cessna, Jerry. *Milk Protein Products and Related Government Policy Issues.* U.S. Department of Agriculture, Agricultural Marketing Service, February 2004, http://www.ams.usda.gov/dairy/mlk_protein_rpt.pdf.

Chavas, J-P., T.L. Cox, and E.V. Jesse. "Spatial Allocation and the Shadow Pricing of Product Characteristics." *Agricultural Economics.* 1998, pp. 1-19.

Chite, Ralph M. *Dairy Policy Issues.* CRS Issue Brief for Congress. Library of Congress, Congressional Research Service, Order Code IB97011, updated July 30, 2003, http://www.ncseonline.org/NLE/CRSreports/03Aug/IB97011.pdf.

Chung, Chanjin, and Harry M. Kaiser. "Do Farmers Get an Equal Bang for Their Buck from Generic Advertising Programs?" *Journal of Agricultural and Resource Economics.* Volume 25, No. 1, July 2000, pp. 147-158.

Cotterill, R.W., and A.W. Franklin. "The Public Interest and Private Economic Power: A Case of the Northeast Interstate Dairy Compact," Food Marketing Policy Center, University of Connecticut, Storrs, CT, 2001.

Cotterill, Ronald W., and Adam N. Rabinowitz. "Analysis of Two Related Milk Price Approaches to Address the Noncompetitive Pricing Problem in the Milk Industry: The 40-40 Consumer Approach and the Farmer and Consumer Fair Share Approach." Food Marketing Policy Center, University of Connecticut, Storrs, CT, January 10, 2003.

Cox, Thomas L., and Jean-Paul Chavas. "An Interregional Analysis of Price Discrimination and Domestic Policy Reform in the U.S. Dairy Sector." *American Journal of Agricultural Economics,* Vol. 83, No. 1, February 2001, pp. 89-106.

Cox, Tom, Bob Cropp, and Will Hughes. "Interregional Analysis of Interstate Dairy Compacts." Marketing and Policy Briefing Paper No. 69, University of Wisconsin-Madison, July 1999.

Cox, Tom, and Hooman Dabidia. "Interregional Impacts of 2002 U.S. Dairy Policies: NE/South/Western Dairy Compacts and Deregulation Scenarios." Paper presented to Looking Ahead...or Looking Behind? 10th Annual Workshop for Dairy Economists and Policy Analysts. Memphis, Tennessee, April 23-24, 2003, http://www.dairy.cornell.edu/CPDMP/Pages/Work-shops/Memphis03/Cox.pdf.

Cropp, Bob. "Dairy Cooperatives and Federal Milk Marketing Orders." Paper presented to Looking Ahead...or Looking Behind? 10th Annual Workshop for Dairy Economists and Policy Analysts. Memphis, Tennessee, April 23-24, 2003, http://www.dairy.cornell.edu/CPDMP/Pages/Work-shops/Memphis03/Cropp.pdf.

Cropp, Bob, and Mark Stephenson. "Dairy Policy Options and Issues for the 2002 Farm Bill." The 2002 Farm Bill: Policy Options and Consequences. The Farm Foundation, 2001, http://www.farmfoundation.org/2002FB/3-3.pdf.

Dobson, W. D., and Paul Christ. *Structural Change in the U.S. Dairy Industry: Growth in Scale, Regional Shifts in Milk Production and Processing, and Internationalism.* Department of Agricultural and Applied Economics, University of Wisconsin-Madison, Staff Paper 438, December 2000.

DuPuis, E. M. "Sub-National State Institutions and the Organization of Agricultural Resource Use: The Case of the Dairy Industry." *Rural Sociology* 58, 1993, pp. 440-460.

Eberle, Phillip R., Kenneth E. Griswold, William C. Peterson, C. Matthew Rendleman and Manish Ruwali. "Economic Impacts of Alternative Dairy Production Systems on the Illinois Economy: A Procedure for Evaluating Alternative Production Systems in IMPLAN." Prepared for presentation at the Missouri Valley Economic Association's 39th Annual Meeting, St. Louis, MO, February 27-March 1, 2003.

Gardner, Bruce L. *American Agriculture in the Twentieth Century—How it Flourished and What It Cost.* Harvard University Press, Cambridge, MA, 2002.

Gilbert, J., and R. Akor. "Increasing Structural Divergence in U.S. Dairying: California and Wisconsin Since 1950." *Rural Sociology* 53, 1988, pp. 56-72.

Hall, Charles L., et al. *Retail and Wholesale Prices for Produce.* AFPC Policy Research Report 93-3. Texas A&M University System, College Station, TX, January 1993.

Hamm, Larry G. *The 1990 Dairy Legislation: An Unfinished Dairy Policy.* Michigan State University, Department of Agricultural Economics, Staff Paper No. 91-06, East Lansing, MI, January 1991.

Harris, Hal. "U.S. Dairy Programs and World Trade Policy Issues" in Looking Ahead. . . or Looking Behind? Proceedings of the 10th Annual Workshop for Dairy Economists and Policy Analysts. Memphis, TN, April 23 and 24, 2003, http://www.dairy.cornell.edu/CPDMP/Pages/Workshops/Memphis03/Harris.pdf.

Harris, J. Michael, Phil R. Kaufman, Steve W. Martinez (coordinator), and Charlene Price. *The U.S. Food Marketing System, 2002—Competition, Coordination, And Technological Innovations Into the 21st Century.* U.S. Department of Agriculture, Economic Research Service, Agricultural Economic Report No. 811, June 2002.

Heien, D.M., and C. RoheimWessels. "The Demand for Dairy Products: Structure, Prediction and Decomposition." *American Journal of Agricultural Economics*, Vol. 70, May 1988, pp. 219-228.

Helmberger, P., and Y. Chen. "Economic Effects of U.S. Dairy Programs." *Journal of Agricultural and Resource Economics*, Vol. 19, December 1994, pp. 225-238.

Huang, K. S. *U.S. Demand for Food: A Complete System of Price and Income Effects*. U.S. Department of Agriculture, Economic Research Service. Technical Bulletin No. 1714, 1985.

Jackson-Smith, Douglas, and Bradford Barham. *The Changing Face of Wisconsin Dairy Farms: A Summary of PATS' Research on Structural Change in the 1990s*. PATS Research Report No. 7, University of Wisconsin-Madison, College of Agricultural and Life Sciences, August 2000.

Jesse, E. "Section 102: The California Make Allowance Issue." University of Wisconsin-Madison, Department of Agricultural Economics Staff Paper No. 46. April 1994.

_____. *U.S. Imports of Concentrated Milk Proteins: What We Know and Don't Know*. Market and Policy Briefing Paper 80. Dept. of Agricultural and Applied Economics, University of Wisconsin-Madison. February, 2003.

Jesse, Edward V. "Facing Up to the Western Dairy Boom." *Rethinking Dairyland: Background for Decisions About Wisconsin's Dairy Industry*, No. 3, September 2002, http://www.aae.wisc.edu/www/pub/dairyland/rd3.pdf.

Kaufman, Phil R. "Consolidation in Food Retailing: Prospects for Consumers & Grocery Suppliers." *Agricultural Outlook*, U.S. Department of Agriculture, Economic Research Service, AGO-273, August 2000, pp. 18-22.

Knutson, Ronald D., Oral Capps, and Robert B. Schwart. "An Assessment of the Experience with and Future of Interstate Dairy Compacts." Looking Ahead . . . or Looking Behind? proceedings of 10th Annual Workshop for Dairy Economists and Policy Analysts. Memphis, TN, April 23-24, 2003, http://www.dairy.cornell.edu/CPDMP/Pages/Workshops/Memphis03/Knutson.pdf.

Kraenzle, Charles A., and E. Eldon Eversull. "Co-ops increase share of farm marketings; share of farm supply sales dips slightly." *Rural Cooperatives*, U.S. Department of Agriculture, Rural Business-Cooperative Service, May/June 2003.

Kuminoff, Nicolai V., Daniel A. Sumner, and George Goldman. *The Measure of California Agriculture, 2000*, University of California, Davis, California Agricultural Issues Center, November 2000.

LaDue, Eddy, Brent Gloy, and Charles Cuykendall. "Future Structure of the Dairy Industry: Historical Trends, Projections and Issues." Cornell Program on Agricultural and Small Business Finance, Department of Applied Economics and Management, Cornell University Agricultural Experiment Station, Ithaca, NY. R.B. 2003-01, June 2003, http://aem.cornell.edu/research/researchpdf/rb0301.pdf.

Lass, Daniel A., Mawunyo Adanu, and P. Geoffrey Allen. "Impacts of the Northeast Dairy Compact on New England Retail Prices," *Agricultural and Resource Economics Review*, 2001, pp. 83-92.

Legislative Analysts Office. *Cal Facts: California Economy and Budget in Perspective*, 1996.

Liebrand, Carolyn. *Structural Change in the Dairy Cooperative Sector, 1992-2000*. U.S. Department of Agriculture, Rural Business-Cooperative Service, RBS Research Report 187, October 2001.

Liebrand, Carolyn Betts, and Karen J. Spatz. *DARIMAC: An Export Marketing Agency-In-Common for Dairy Cooperatives*. U.S. Department of Agriculture, Agricultural Cooperative Service, ACS Research Report 126, December 1993.

Lin, Biing-Hwan, J.N. Variyam, J. Allshouse, and J. Cromartie. *Food and Agricultural Commodity Consumption in the United States: Looking Ahead to 2020*. U.S. Department of Agriculture, Economic Research Service. Agricultural Economic Report No. 820, February 2003.

Ling, K. Charles. "Dairy Co-ops Continue Dominant Role in Marketing Nation's Milk." *Rural Cooperatives*, U.S. Department of Agriculture, Rural Business-Cooperative Service, March/April 2004.

_____. *Marketing Operations of Dairy Cooperatives*. U.S. Department of Agriculture, Rural Business-Cooperative Service, RBS Research Report 173, June 1999.

Manchester, Alden C. *The Public Role in the Dairy Economy*. Westview Press, Boulder, CO, 1983.

Manchester, Alden C., and Don P. Blayney. *Milk Pricing in the United States*. U.S. Department of Agriculture, Economic Research Service. Agriculture Information Bulletin No. 761, February 2001.

_____. *The Structure of Dairy Markets: Past, Present, Future*. U.S. Department of Agriculture, Economic Research Service. Agricultural Economic Report No. 757, September 1997.

Matulich, Scott C. "Efficiencies in Large-Scale Dairying: Incentives for Future Structural Change." *American Journal of Agricultural Economics*, Vol. 60, No. 4, November 1978, pp. 642-647.

McElroy, Robert, Roger Strickland, Jim Ryan, Chris McGath, Robert Green, Ken Erickson, and William McBride. *Agricultural Income and Finance*

Outlook. U.S. Department of Agriculture, Economic Research Service, Agricultural Income and Finance Situation and Outlook No. 79, September 2002.

Meadows, D. L. *Dynamics of Commodity Production Cycles*. Wright-Allen Press, Cambridge, MA, 1970.

Miller, James. "Tortoises Triumph: Gradual Changes Transform the Dairy Industry." *Agricultural Outlook*. U.S. Department of Agriculture, Economic Research Service, December 2002, pp. 8-10.

Mishra, Ashok K., Hisham S. El-Osta, Michell J. Morehart, James D. Johnson, and Jeffrey W. Hopkins. *Income, Wealth, and the Economic Well-Being of Farm Households*. U.S. Department of Agriculture, Economic Research Service. Agricultural Economic Report No. 812, July 2002.

Morehart, M., Betsey Kuhn, and Susan Offutt. "A Fair Income for Farmers?" *Agricultural Outlook*, U.S. Department of Agriculture, Economic Research Service, May 2000, pp. 22-26.

Moschini, Giancarlo. "The Cost Structure of of Ontario Dairy Farms: A Microeconomic Analysis." *Canadian Journal of Agricultural Economics*, Vol. 36, 1998, pp. 187-206.

Natcher, W. C., and R. D. Weaver. "Price Volatility in the US Dairy Sector: Due to Week-of-Month Effects?" Selected paper presented at the Annual Meetings, American Agricultural Economics Association, Chicago, IL. 2001.

National Milk Producers Federation. *Milk Protein Imports: Impacts on U.S. Dairy Producers*. April 2001.

Newbury, D. M. G., and J. E. Stiglitz. *The Theory of Commodity Price Stabilization: A Study in the Economics of Risk*. Clarendon Press, Oxford, England, 1981.

Nicholson, Charles, and Thomas Fiddaman. "Dairy Policy and Price Volatility." Paper presented to Looking Ahead...or Looking Behind? 10th Annual Workshop for Dairy Economists and Policy Analysts. Memphis, Tennessee, April 23-24, 2003, http://www.dairy.cornell.edu/CPDMP/Pages/Workshops/Memphis03/Nicholson.pdf.

Nicholson, C.F., B. Resosudarmo, and F.W. Wackernagel. "Impacts of the Northeast Interstate Dairy Compact on New England Milk Supply," *Agricultural and Resource Economics Review*, 2001, pp. 93-103.

Nicholson, C.F., and R. Wackernagel, "Impacts of the Compact on New England Milkshed Composition," in *The Northeast Interstate Dairy Compact: Milk Market Impacts*. Charles F. Nicholson, editor. University of Vermont Research Report 73, Burlington, VT, 2000.

Northeast Dairy Compact Commission, http://www.dairycompact.org.

Nubern, Chris A. "Evaluating Changes in Demand for Dairy Products," *U.S. Dairy Markets & Outlook,* Vol. 3, No. 2, April 1998.

Outlaw, Joe L., David P. Anderson, and James W. Richardson. "Impacts of Removing Current Federal Regulations on U.S. representative Dairy Farms" Paper presented to Looking Ahead...or Looking Behind? 10th Annual Workshop for Dairy Economists and Policy Analysts. Memphis, TN, April 23-24, 2003, http://www.dairy.cornell.edu/CPDMP/Pages/Workshops/Memphis03/Outlaw.pdf.

Outlaw, Joe L., Ronald D. Knutson, George B. Marek, Brian J. Eiting, Robert B. Schwart, Jr., and Jayantha R. Perera. *A Case Study of Retail Pricing Strategies in Two Texas Cities*. AFPC Policy Research Report 94-3. Texas A&M University System, College Station, TX, July 26, 1994, p. 13.

Padberg, D.I., Ron Knutson, and S. Hussain Ali Jafri. *Retail Food Pricing: Horizontal and Vertical Determinants*. AFPC Policy Research Report 93-1. Texas A&M University System, College Station, TX, January 1993, p. 12.

Pratt, J. E., and M. W. Stephenson. "Motives for Storing Manufactured Dairy Products." Paper presented at "Price Instability and Risk Management in the Dairy Industry," August 20-21, 1998, Alexandria, VA, 1998.

Price, J. Michael. *Effects of U.S. Dairy Policies on Markets for Milk and Dairy Products*. U.S. Department of Agriculture, Economic Research Service, Technical Bulletin No. 1910, March 2004.

Putnam, Judy, and Jane Allshouse. "Trends in U.S. Per Capita Consumption of Dairy Products, 1909 to 2001." *Amber Waves*. U.S. Department of Agriculture, Economic Research Service, June 2003.

Reynolds, Bruce J. *Cooperative Marketing Agencies-in-Common*. U.S. Department of Agriculture, Agricultural Cooperative Service, ACS Research Report 127, January 1994.

Richardson, J. W., J. L. Outlaw, D. P. Anderson, J. D. Sartwelle, III, P. Feldman, K. Schumann, J. M. Raulston, S. L. Klose, R. B. Schwart, Jr., and P. Zimmel. "Representative Farms Economic Outlook for the January 2003 FAPRI/AFPC Baseline." Texas Agricultural Experiment Station, Department of Agricultural Economics, Texas A&M University, College Station, TX, Agricultural and Food Policy Center Working Paper 03-1, March 2003.

Salathe, Larry. "The Implications of Offsetting Adjustments in Government Purchase Prices for Butter and Nonfat Dry Milk." *The Journal of Agricultural Economics Research*. Vol. 45, No. 1, 1993, pp. 18-26.

Salathe, L., and J.M. Price. "Implications of raising the nonfat solids standards for beverage milk." *Southern Journal of Agricultural Economics*, Vol. 24, December 1992, pp. 197-209.

Schmit, Todd M., and Harry M. Kaiser. Measuring the Impacts of Generic Fluid Milk and Cheese Advertising: *A Time-Varying Parameter Application*.

NICPRE 02-03 R.B. 2002-06. Department of Applied Economics and Management, Cornell University, Ithaca, NY, May 2002.

Short, Sara D. *Characteristics and Production Costs of U.S. Dairy Operations*. U.S. Department of Agriculture, Economic Research Service. Statistical Bulletin No. SB-974-6, February 2004, http://www.ers.usda.gov/publications/sb974-6/.

Southard, Leland (coordinator). *Livestock, Dairy, and Poultry Outlook*. U.S. Department of Agriculture, Economic Research Service. Electronic Outlook Report (various), http://www.ers.usda.gov/publications/ldp/.

Sparks Companies, Inc. *Imports of MPCs, Casein and Caseinates and Market Impacts—A Special Study for the U.S. Coalition for Nutritional Ingredients*. May, 2003.

Stephenson, Mark. "Technology, Demand, and Lost Data." Presentation to Forces Shaping the Dairy Industry Workshop, U.S. Department of Agriculture, Economic Research Service, Washington, DC, September 25, 2002, http://www.farmfoundation.org/projects/03-36DairyPolicyForumpresentations.htm.

Sumner, D.A., and N.L.Wilson. "The Development of California Milk Marketing Laws: In Pursuit of an Adequate Supply of Healthful Milk." Paper presented at Agricultural History Symposium, Mississippi State, MS, June 1999.

Sumner, D.A., and C.A. Wolf. "Quotas Without Supply Control: Effects of Dairy Quota Policy in California." *American Journal of Agricultural Economics,* Vol. 78, 1996, pp. 354-366.

Tillison, Jim. "What's the answer for MPC imports?" *Hoard's Dairyman.* April 10, 2002, p. 271.

Tomek, William G., and Kenneth L. Robinson. *Agricultural Product Prices.* Cornell University Press, Ithaca, NY, 1972.

U.S. Congress. "Review of the Dairy Termination Program and Other Ongoing Dairy Program Initiatives Mandated in the Food Security Act of 1985." Hearing before the Subcommittee on Livestock, Dairy and Poultry, Committee on Agriculture, House of Representatives, 100th Congress, 1st Session, Washington, DC, March 4, 1987.

U.S. Department of Agriculture, *Agricultural Statistics Database,* http://www.nass.usda.gov:81/ipedb/.

U.S. Department of Agriculture, Agricultural Marketing Service. *Federal Milk Marketing Order Reform, New England et al. Final Decision—Regulatory Impact Analysis*, March 1999, http://www.ams.usda.gov/fmor/ria.pdf.

_____. "Federal Milk Marketing Orders," http://www.ams.usda.gov/dairy/orders.htm.

_____. *Federal Milk Order Market Statistics*, Annual Summary (various years).

_____. "Milk Marketing Order Statistics," http://www.ams.usda.gov/dyfmos/mib/price_form_2003.htm.

_____. *Packaged Fluid Milk Sales in Federal Milk Order Markets: By Size and Type of Container and Distribution Method During November 2001*. December 2002.

_____. *Report to Congress on the National Dairy Promotion and Research Program and the National Fluid Milk Processor Promotion Program*. July 1, 2002. http://www.ams.usda.gov/dairy/prb/rtc_2002/total_rtc_2002.pdf.

U.S. Department of Agriculture, Economic Research Service. *Dairy: Background for 1985 Farm Legislation*, Agricultural Information Bulletin No. 474.

_____. "Farm Financial Management Data: Selected Farm Operator Household Financial Characteristics," http://www.ers.usda.gov/Data/farmfinancialmgmt/hhf_typmenu.htm.

_____. *Food Consumption (Per Capita) Data System*. http://www.ers.usda.gov/data/foodconsumption/.

_____. "Links to the General Economy and Agriculture," Food and Nutrition Assistance Programs and the General Economy briefing room, http://ers.usda.gov/Briefing/GeneralEconomy/linkages.htm.

_____. *Livestock, Dairy, and Poultry Outlook*. LDP-M-108, June 24, 2003.

U.S. Department of Agriculture, Foreign Agriculture Service. "FACT SHEET: Dairy Export Incentive Program," http://www.fas.usda.gov/info/factsheets/deip.html.

U.S. Department of Agriculture, National Agricultural Statistics Service. *Census of Agriculture*, http://www.nass.usda.gov/census/.

_____. *Dairy Products Annual Summary*. Various issues.

_____. Milk Cows and Production. 1950-1998.

_____. *Milk Production*, February 2002.

U.S. Department of Agriculture, Rural Business-Cooperative Service. *Cooperatives in the Dairy Industry*, Cooperative Information Report 1, Section 16, July 2002.

U.S. Department of Commerce, Economic and Statistics Administration, Bureau of the Census. *Concentration Ratios in Manufacturing.* 1997 Economic Census—Manufacturing. June 2001, and previous issues.

U.S. General Accounting Office. *Dairy Industry Information on Milk Prices and Changing Market Structure.* GAO-01-561, June 2001.

_____. *Dairy Products: Imports, Domestic Production, and Regulation of Ultra-filtered Milk.* GAO-01-326. March 2001.

U.S. International Trade Commission. *Conditions of Competition for Milk Protein Products in the U.S. Market.* Investigation No. 332-453, USITC Publication 3692, May 2004.

Wisconsin Department of Agriculture Trade and Consumer Protection. *Wisconsin Dairy Facts*, various years.

Wisconsin State Journal, September 1993.

Wolf, Christopher A., and Larry G. Hamm. "The Role of Cooperatives in Milk Marketing." Paper presented at the annual meeting of the American Agricultural Economics Association, Salt Lake City, UT, August 2-5, 1998.

Appendix A—Mandate for Dairy Study from the 2002 Farm Security and Rural Investment Act, H.R. 2646

SEC. 1507. STUDY OF NATIONAL DAIRY POLICY.
(a) STUDY REQUIRED.—The Secretary of Agriculture shall conduct a comprehensive economic evaluation of the potential direct and indirect effects of the various elements of the national dairy policy, including an examination of the effect of the national dairy policy on—
(1) farm price stability, farm profitability and viability, and local rural economies in the United States;
(2) child, senior, and low-income nutrition programs, including impacts on schools and institutions participating in the programs, on program recipients, and other factors; and
(3) the wholesale and retail cost of fluid milk, dairy farms, and milk utilization.
(b) REPORT.—Not later than 1 year after the date of enactment of this Act, the Secretary shall submit to the Committee on Agriculture of the House of Representatives and the Committee on Agriculture, Nutrition, and Forestry of the Senate a report describing the results of the study required by this section.
(c) NATIONAL DAIRY POLICY DEFINED.—In this section, the term "national dairy policy" means the dairy policy of the United States as evidenced by the following policies and programs:
(1) Federal milk marketing orders issued under section 8c of the Agricultural Adjustment Act (7 U.S.C. 608c), reenacted with amendments by the Agricultural Marketing Act of 1937.
(2) Interstate dairy compacts (including proposed compacts described in H.R. 1827 and S. 1157, as introduced in the 107th Congress).
(3) Over-order premiums and State pricing programs.
(4) Direct payments to milk producers.
(5) Federal milk price support program established under section 1401.
(6) Export programs regarding milk and dairy products, such as the dairy export incentive program established under section 153 of the Food Security Act of 1985 (15 U.S.C. 713a–14).
SEC. 1508. STUDIES OF EFFECTS OF CHANGES IN APPROACH TO NATIONAL DAIRY POLICY AND FLUID MILK IDENTITY STANDARDS.
(a) FEDERAL DAIRY POLICY CHANGES.—The Secretary of Agriculture-shall conduct a study of the effects of—
(1) terminating all Federal programs relating to price support and supply management for milk; and
(2) granting the consent of Congress to cooperative efforts by States to manage milk prices and supply.

Appendix B—Summary of Legislation Affecting National Dairy Policy

Legislation	Federal milk marketing orders	Interstate dairy compacts	Over-order premiums and State pricing	Direct payments	Federal milk price support	Export programs
Agricultural Adjustment Act of 1933	Marketing agreements permitted--progenitor of orders				An ad hoc program loosely based on Land O'Lakes butter purchase activities	
Agricultural Adjustment Act amendments, 1935					Section 22 import quota authority given to the President	
Young Act (1935)			California establishes minimum producer pricing			
Agricultural Marketing Act of 1937	Authorized and clarified marketing orders to replace agreements if necessary					
Desmond Act (1937)			California extends minimum producer pricing to all milk classes			
Milk Control Act (1937)			Milk industry regulation made permanent in Pennsylvania			
Agricultural Act of 1949					Underlying foundations of current milk price support program codified	
Agricultural Trade Development and Assistance Act of 1954 (PL-480)						Groundwork for use of surplus commodities in foreign and domestic food programs

Continued on page 100

Appendix B—Summary of Legislation Affecting National Dairy Policy—continued

Legislation	Federal milk marketing orders	Interstate dairy compacts	Over-order premiums and State pricing	Direct payments	Federal milk price support	Export programs
Gonsalves Milk Pooling Act (1967)			California establishes statewide pooling of producer revenues using base, overbase, and quota system			
Milk Control Act (1967), amended			Pennsylvania Milk Marketing Board (PMMB) becomes independent agency (can pay over-order premiums)			
Agriculture and Food Act of 1981					Support level written into legislation, no longer based on parity, and linked to Govt. program costs and quantities purchased	
Omnibus Budget Reconciliation Act of 1982					Support level frozen and assessments to pay for program instituted (on farmers)	
Dairy and Tobacco Adjustment Act of 1983				Milk Diversion program voluntary supply mgmt.	Repeal of farmer assessment	
Food Security Act of 1985	Class I differentials written directly in legislation			Authorized second supply mgmt. program Dairy Termination (Herd Buyout)		DEIP authorized

Continued on page 101

Appendix B—Summary of Legislation Affecting National Dairy Policy—continued

Legislation	Federal milk marketing orders	Interstate dairy compacts	Over-order premiums and State pricing	Direct payments	Federal milk price support	Export programs
Food, Agriculture, Conservation, and Trade Act of 1990					Fixed support price at $10.10 per hundredweight	DEIP extended
Uruguay Round Agreements Act of 1994					Section 22 quotas replaced by TRQs	Committed U.S. to reduce subsidized exports of dairy products
Federal Agriculture Improvement Act of 1996	Reform marketing orders by reducing number of orders, revisit pricing rules	Authorized Northeast Interstate Dairy Compact			Milk support purchase program to end after support price goes to $9.90 per cwt (1999)	DEIP continued subject to WTO commitments
Agriculture, Rural Development, Food and Drug, and Related Agencies Appropriation Act, 1999				Dairy Market Loss I (Ad hoc emergency assistance to milk producers)	Extended 1 yr. at $9.90 per cwt	
Agriculture, Rural Development, Food and Drug, and Related Agencies Appropriation Act, 2000				Dairy Market Loss II	Extended 1 yr. at $9.90 per cwt	
Agriculture, Rural Development, Food and Drug, and Related Agencies Appropriation Act 2001				Dairy Market Loss III	Extended 1 yr. at $9.90 per cwt	
Food Security and Rural Investment Act of 2002				MILC direct payment program	Milk price support program reinstituted as longer term program at fixed $9.90 per cwt	DEIP extended

Note: Entries in **bold** refer to State laws.
Source: Compiled by USDA, Economic Research Service.

Appendix C—FAPRI and FAPSIM Baseline Values for Selected Dairy Industry Indicators

FAPRI		2003	2004	2005	2006	2007	Average
Milk production	billion pounds	171.2	172.8	174.5	175.4	176.7	174.1
All-milk price	dollars per cwt	12.19	12.24	12.27	12.52	12.58	12.36
MILC payments	dollars per cwt	1.22	1.18	1.16	0.00	0.00	0.71
Cow numbers	thousand head	9,067	9,011	8,965	8,896	8,841	8,956
Wholesale price							
cheese	dollars per pound	1.25	1.25	1.26	1.28	1.29	1.27
butter	dollars per pound	1.19	1.25	1.26	1.33	1.35	1.28
nonfat dry milk	dollars per pound	0.84	0.81	0.81	0.81	0.8	10.82
Per capita consumption							
cheese	pounds	30.1	30.5	30.8	31.0	31.2	30.7
butter	pounds	4.7	4.6	4.6	4.5	4.5	4.6
nonfat dry milk	pounds	3.3	3.4	3.4	3.4	3.5	3.4
fluid	pounds	207.8	207.9	207.5	206.4	205.3	207.0
Govenment outlays	million dollars, fiscal year	2,586.4	1,524.4	1,501.3	579.9	268.0	1,292.0

FAPSIM		2002	2003	2004	2005	2006	2007	Average
Milk production	billion pounds	169.2	171.8	173.2	174.9	176.7	178.6	174.1
All-milk price	dollars per cwt	12.47	11.84	12.79	13.15	13.40	13.67	12.89
MILC payments	billion dollars	0.90	1.20	0.90	0.60	0.00	0.00	0.60
Cow numbers	thousand head	9,202	9,080	8,739	8,578	8,497	8,371	8,745
Wholesale price								
cheese	dollars per pound	1.20	1.17	1.29	1.33	1.35	1.38	1.29
butter	dollars per pound	0.89	0.73	0.92	1.00	1.07	1.14	0.96
nonfat dry milk	dollars per pound	1.04	1.03	1.04	1.04	1.04	1.04	1.04
Per capita consumption								
cheese	pounds	29.8	29.6	30.4	30.8	31.2	31.7	30.6
butter	pounds	5.5	5.7	5.7	5.7	5.7	5.8	5.7
nonfat dry milk	pounds	3.6	3.7	3.8	3.9	3.9	4.0	3.8
fluid	pounds	195.5	194.0	191.2	188.1	184.3	181.6	189.1
Government outlays	million dollars, fiscal year	240.0	2,353.6	1,284.6	1,021.0	342.8	320.6	927.1

Note: The MILC payments are measured differently in the two models, per cwt in FAPRI, total in FAPSIM.

Source: Brown (2003) and Price (2004).

Appendix D—Overview of Nutrition Programs

U.S. Government food assistance programs influence demand for dairy products. They target different populations with different needs. The Food Stamp Program and the Special Supplemental Nutrition Program for Women, Infants, and Children (WIC), together with the child nutrition programs—the National School Lunch, the School Breakfast, the Child and Adult Care Food, the Summer Food, and the Special Milk Programs—are likely to be the most affected by changes in the national dairy policy.

The **Food Stamp Program** enables low-income participants to obtain a more nutritious diet by issuing monthly allotments of coupons or Electronic Benefits redeemable for food at authorized retail food stores. The Food Stamp Program is available to most households that meet income and asset criteria. Food Stamps can be used to purchase most types of foods including dairy products, and recipients choose the combinations of approved foods they purchase.

Food stamp benefit levels are based on the cost of a market basket containing multiple food items that models how a low-income household can achieve a low-cost diet plan that meets dietary standards. Benefits levels are sensitive to changes in the price of dairy products since milk accounts for about 10 percent of the value of the market basket.

The Food Stamp Program entitles those who meet the eligibility criteria to receive benefits, so changes in dairy product prices do not affect the provision of benefits. An increase (decrease) in the price of dairy products resulting from a change in dairy policy would increase (decrease) the cost of the market basket resulting in an increase (decrease) in cost of the Food Stamp Program to the Federal Government. In addition, the purchasing power of individual food stamp households may be affected to the degree that they purchase dairy products with their food stamps.

The **Special Supplemental Nutrition Program for Women, Infants, and Children (WIC)** provides nutritious supplemental foods at no cost to low-income pregnant and postpartum women, as well as infants and children up to their fifth birthday who are determined by health professionals to be nutritionally at risk. Participants can redeem WIC food vouchers at retail food stores for specific foods that are rich in the nutrients typically lacking in the diets of the target population. In fiscal year 2000, dairy purchases accounted for almost 40 percent of the total (after rebates) WIC food costs.

WIC is a discretionary grant program funded by appropriations law on an annual basis. Therefore, the number of participants that can be served each year depends upon the annual appropriation and the cost of operating the program—the program provides services to as many eligible people as funding allows. Consequently, an increase in WIC food costs resulting from an increase in dairy prices will not increase Federal costs. However, an increase in the cost of the WIC food packages, if not offset by the Government, would result in fewer people being served if the composition of the food packages remain unchanged. In the case of the Northeast Interstate Dairy Compact (NEIDC), higher dairy prices did not increase government costs or reduce benefits. The NEIDC compensated the WIC program in the six New England States $3.8 million from 1997 through 2000 for increased milk costs due to the Compact.

The **National School Lunch Program** provides lunches to children in public schools, nonprofit private schools, and residential child care institutions. Schools receive cash and entitlement commodities from USDA to offset the cost of food service. In return, the schools must serve lunches that meet Federal nutritional requirements and offer free or reduced-price lunches to needy children. Schools that participate in the National School Lunch Program must offer milk with the lunch. Milk is also one of the options for a snack in the afternoon snack service in the National School Lunch Program.

The commodity subsidy is indexed to the Price Index of Foods Used in Schools and Institutions. This index is computed using five major food components in the Bureau of Labor Statistics Producer Price Index— including dairy products. Increases in the indices resulting from higher dairy prices would result in higher government costs. The NEIDC compensated the six New England States $662,606 for the 1998-1999 and 1999-2000 school years for increases in milk prices incurred by the National School Lunch, School Breakfast, and Special Milk Programs.

The **School Breakfast Program** provides low-cost breakfasts to school children, with students from low-income families receiving free or reduced-price meals. USDA provides schools with cash assistance to offset the cost of food service. In return, the schools must serve breakfasts that meet Federal nutrition standards. Milk must be offered at each breakfast, and may be served as a beverage, on cereal, or both. Reimbursements in the School Breakfast Program are indexed to a Consumer Price Index, and increases in the index resulting from higher dairy prices would result in higher government costs.

The **Special Milk Program** provides funding for milk in public and nonprofit schools, child care centers, summer camps, and similar institutions that do not participate in any other federally assisted nutrition program. Participating sites provide milk either free or at low cost to all children. USDA reimburses participating schools and institutions for part of the cost of the milk served to children. Reimbursements are indexed to the Producer Price Index for Fluid Milk Products.

The **Child and Adult Care Food Program** (CACFP) provides healthy meals and snacks to children in participating child care centers and in family and group day care homes as well as to adults in adult day care centers. In child care and adult day care centers, children and adults from low-income families are eligible for free or reduced-price meals. Independent centers and sponsoring agencies receive cash reimbursement for each meal served. Child care centers participating in the CACFP have the option of receiving commodities or cash in lieu of commodities. Milk must be offered at each meal served in the child care segment of the CACFP and with the adult breakfasts and lunches. Milk is also one of the options for a snack in the CACFP. Cash reimbursements for meals and commodity subsidies are indexed to one of the Consumer Price Indices.

The **Summer Food Service Program** provides free meals to children (age 18 and under) and handicapped people over age 18 during school vacations in areas where at least half of the children are from low-income households. Milk must be offered at each meal and is an option for the snacks served in the program. The program is operated at the local level by sponsors who are reimbursed by USDA. Sponsors are reimbursed for each meal served and for their documented operating costs. Reimbursements in the program are indexed to a Consumer Price Index.

USDA also buys and supplies surplus food to the National School Lunch Program, the Child and Adult Care Food Program, and the Summer Food Service Program. Schools participating in the National School Lunch Program receive commodity foods, called "entitlement" foods. Schools can also get "bonus" commodities, through USDA's price support and surplus removal programs. Entitlement foods available for these Child Nutrition Programs in the 2002-2003 school year include cheese and nonfat dry milk. The type and quantity of bonus commodities distributed by USDA in a given year is dictated by agricultural surpluses and market conditions.

Glossary

All-milk price—The average price of all the milk sold to plants and dealers. The price received by the producer is lower, reflecting handling and other marketing costs.

Balancing—A service, usually provided by cooperative associations of milk producers, that involves directing milk movements between producers' farms and handlers' plants and diverting supplies in excess of handlers' needs to alternative outlets such as manufactured dairy product plants.

Blend price—A weighted average price based on the proportion of Grade A milk in a pool allocated to each of the use classes. Producers participating in a pool receive its blend price with adjustments for butterfat content and plant location.

Casein—The major protein contained in milk and the primary protein in cheese. Also, a protein curd or dried product made from milk casein curd.

Class I differential—The amount added to the Class I price mover (the higher of the advanced Class III or Class IV pricing factors) in a Federal milk marketing order to obtain a county's Class I price. Class I differentials vary by location, with a differential specified for each county in the country. The purpose of the Class I differentials is to assure an adequate supply of milk for fluid use by encouraging movement of grade A milk for fluid use from production areas to fluid milk plants.

Classified pricing—A structure of prices that differ according to category of use; the Federal order pricing system under which regulated processors pay for Grade A milk according to the class in which it is used.

Commodity Credit Corporation (CCC)—A wholly owned federal corporation within the U.S. Department of Agriculture, subject to the direction of the Secretary of Agriculture. Price support purchases, the Milk Income Loss Contract (MILC) program, and many other commodity program activities involving expenditures of funds are conducted by the CCC.

Compact—An agreement between or among States to regulate some area of commerce. A compact must be approved in identical form by each party (State) to it and authorized by the U.S. Congress.

Cooperative—A firm that is owned by its farmer-members, is operated for their benefit, and distributes earnings on the basis of volume of milk.

Dairy Export Incentive Program (DEIP)—Helps exporters of U.S. dairy products meet prevailing world prices for targeted dairy products and destinations by provding cash bonuses to exporters, allowing them to sell certain U.S. dairy products at prices lower than the costs of acquiring them.

Economies of scale/size— Economies of scale are increasing returns as all inputs are increased in equal proportions. Economies of size are increasing returns as use of inputs is expanded in least-cost combinations.

Elasticity—A numerical measure of the proportional change in quantity demanded (or quantity supplied) in response to a change in price or income.

FAPRI—**F**ood and **A**gricultural **P**olicy **R**esearch **I**nstitute. Refers both to the research institute, located at both the University of Missouri and Iowa State University, and, in this report, the modeling system used by this research institute to analyze the effects of dairy policy.

FAPSIM—**F**ood and **A**gricultural **P**olicy **SIM**ulator. FAPSIM is an annual econometric model of the U.S. agricultural sector developed by the USDA's Economic Research Service and used to simulate the effects of different policies.

Farm Act—The omnibus agricultural legislation that sets farm policy for a period of 4 or 5 years.

Federal milk marketing order—A regulation issued by the Secretary of Agriculture specifying minimum prices and conditions for the purchase of milk from dairy farmers within a specified geographic area.

FLIPSIM—**F**arm **L**evel **I**ncome and **P**olicy **SIM**ulator. FLIPSIM is a simulation model developed at Texas A&M University used to simulate the economic activities of a representative or actual farm.

Fluid grade (Grade A) milk—Milk produced under sanitary conditions that qualify it for fluid consumption. Only Grade A milk is regulated under Federal milk marketing orders.

Fluid milk—Packaged dairy products used as beverage milks.

Fluid products—A term traditionally used to define products including beverage milks, fluid cream items, and drinkable yogurts.

Grade A milk—Also called fluid grade milk. Milk produced and processed under the strictest sanitary regulations prescribed, inspected and approved by public health authorities. Milk used in any product intended for consumption in fluid form must meet this inspection standard.

Grade B milk—Also called manufacturing grade milk. Milk produced and processed with sanitary regulations prescribed, inspected, and approved by public health authorities for milk to be used for manufactured products only. Not to be confused with "milk used in manufacturing," which can include grade A milk.

Handlers—Generally refers to fluid milk processors but can include manufacturing plants and cooperatives that supply fluid processor needs.

Mailbox price—The price actually received by producers. Includes all payments received for milk sold and all costs associated with the milk.

Make allowance—The allowance to cover the cost of manufacturing that is administratively set to attain CCC purchase prices for butter, nonfat dry milk, and cheese that will enable manufacturing plants to pay, on average, the support price of milk to farmers.

Manufactured dairy products—Includes all dairy products except fluid milks: all cheeses, butter, evaporated whole milk, condensed whole milk, condensed skim milk, whole milk powder, nonfat dry milk, ice cream, ice cream mix, frozen desserts, creams, and whey products.

Manufacturers—Generally refers to the producers of cheese, butter, nonfat dry milk, and other storable dairy products.

Manufacturing milk—Grade B milk or the Grade A milk used in the production of manufactured dairy products.

Market power—The ability of buyers or sellers to influence prices above or below the prices that would have been set in a competitive market.

Milkfat—The fat normally occurring in cow milk. Milkfat consists of short-chain fatty acids that make it easy to digest. Also referred to as butterfat.

Milk Income Loss Contract (MILC)—Compensates dairy producers through direct payments when domestic prices fall below a specified level. Payments are made to a producer up to a maximum of 2.4 million pounds of milk produced per fiscal year.

Milk marketing area—A geographically defined fluid milk demand area for purposes of Federal milk marketing regulations. If a designated portion of a handler's milk is sold in the milk marketing area, all milk of that handler is "pooled."

Milk protein concentrate (MPC)—Protein product derived from skim milk.

Milk-based fractions—Separated milk components with specific functional properties. By separating milk into different fractions, processors can select the specific functional and nutritional qualities needed for a particular food product.

Multiple component pricing—A way of pricing milk that determines its value based on the values of butterfat and nonfat solids (nonfat dry milk, protein, lactose, or other nonfat solids) used in manufactured dairy products. Component values are related to the prices of butter, cheese, and nonfat dry milk.

Natural cheese—Cheese made directly from milk (or whey in some instances). Processed cheese is made by combining natural cheese with other ingredients, heating and mixing them to make a creamy, smooth product.

Nonfat dry milk (NDM or NFDM)—Product obtained by removing water from pasteurized skim milk. Also referred to as skimmed milk powder (SMP) in international markets.

Northeast Interstate Dairy Compact (NEIDC)—A formal agreement between the six New England States, enacted through State and Federal legislation, that allowed for the establishment of a regional pricing mechanism for fluid milk sold in the New England States.

Over-order premium—Payment or price above Federal (or California's) order minimum prices. Over-order premiums that are generated by the market could result from costs of services provided to handlers, tightened supply conditions, or market power. State-mandated over-order premiums regulate payments or prices above Federal order minimum prices.

Parity price—The price which gives a unit of a commodity the same purchasing power today as it had in a base period.

Pooling (revenue, price)—A method for determining how revenues generated in a market are returned to producers. With a classified pricing system such as that used in Federal and State orders, processors pay different prices for milk in each category of use. Producers are paid a weighted average, or "blend," price for all uses of milk in a particular order or market.

Processors—Generally refers to firms that process raw Grade A milk into fluid dairy products.

Raw milk—Farm milk that has not been treated in any way. Raw milk is not pasteurized, separated, standardized, or homogenized.

Skim solids—The solids in milk other than milk fat; e.g., protein, lactose, and minerals. Sometimes referred to as nonfat solids or solids-not-fat (SNF).

Soft products—A category of manufactured products with relatively short shelf life; i.e., cottage cheese, sour cream, ice cream, yogurt, buttermilk, etc.

Solids-not-fat—See skim solids.

Supply management—Variety of plans that attempt to keep milk production—either nationally or in a specific market—from exceeding commercial market needs. Can be used as an alternative to low prices as a way to control production in periods of surplus or as a long-term approach to pricing.

Tariff-rate quota (TRQ)—A two-level tariff where the tariff rate charged depends on the volume of imports. A lower (in-quota) tariff is charged on imports within the quota volume and a higher (over-quota) tariff is charged on imports in excess of the quota volume.

Utilization rates—The relative use of each class of milk in a region or order.